GOODNESS *and* LIGHT
READINGS FOR ADVENT AND CHRISTMAS

GOODNESS
and
LIGHT

READINGS FOR
ADVENT AND CHRISTMAS

*Michael Leach, James Keane,
Doris Goodnough, editors*

ORBIS BOOKS
Maryknoll, New York 10545

Second Printing, September 2015

Founded in 1970, Orbis Books endeavors to publish works that enlighten the mind, nourish the spirit, and challenge the conscience. The publishing arm of the Maryknoll Fathers and Brothers, Orbis seeks to explore the global dimensions of the Christian faith and mission, to invite dialogue with diverse cultures and religious traditions, and to serve the cause of reconciliation and peace. The books published reflect the views of their authors and do not represent the official position of the Maryknoll Society. To learn more about Maryknoll and Orbis Books, please visit our website at www.maryknollsociety.org.

Sources and acknowledgments on pages 258-262 represent an extension of the copyright page.

Manufactured in the United States of America.
Design: Roberta Savage

Library of Congress Cataloging-in-Publication Data

On file with publisher.

ISBN 978-1-62698-123-2

The child, the child
Sleeping in the night
He will bring us goodness and light

—Noël Regney and Gloria Shayne Baker,
Do You Hear What I Hear?

For those who prefer to follow these readings on a daily basis throughout Advent, dates are included for each selection in this book. Because Advent begins on a different calendar date each year, the dates provided account for every possible day within the season of Advent and Epiphany.

Contents

Contents

Contents

Contents

GOODNESS AND LIGHT

January 1
ROWAN WILLIAMS
In Congo or in Croydon, God Is There for Us
page 227

January 2
MAYA ANGELOU
Amazing Peace
page 233

January 3
ERNESTO CARDENAL
The Shepherds of Bethlehem
page 234

January 4
EVELYN UNDERHILL
Missa Cantata
page 244

January 5
OSCAR ROMERO
If Christ Had Become Incarnate Now
page 247

January 6
JOYCE RUPP
Remembering the Sacred Presence of the One Who Dwells among Us
page 250

Contents

INTRODUCTION

Then God said, "Let there be light," and there was light. God saw that the light was good, and he separated it from the dark."

—GENESIS 1: 3-4

You are all the children of light, and the children of the day: we are not of the night, nor of darkness.

—1 THESSALONIANS 5:5

This is not a book but a neighborhood of good hearted people waking up from the dark. A neighborhood of people just like you, all of us opening curtains of grace and letting in the morn. A community of saints who don't yet know how much we shine but are about to be blinded by a star so bright that all we will see is goodness and light.

At least for a little while.

Isn't that the purpose of celebrating Advent and Christmas every year? All of us need to keep on remembering who and where we really are. We forget that we are children of the light, and that we live and move and have our being in the everlasting love that is God. In spite of our suffering or sorrow, comfort and joy is, as Tennyson wrote, "closer . . . than breathing and nearer than hands and feet." No matter how guilty we feel, we are not of the dark but of the light. We are not lost in sin but hidden in God who insists we are good.

God's light shines in the darkness, and always will, but the darkness just can't get it. We often think we are alone and cold and separate from the light but, thank God, Christmas comes every year to remind us that we never left the bosom of love where we always are, where beats eternal the heart of mercy, gratitude, and joy.

The women and men who wrote the selections in this book are our neighbors. They, too, are often fooled by the dark, and here take the time to reflect on the goodness and light that Advent and Christmas represent. They open the pages of their individual spiritual journeys to cast a little light on the paths of us all. You know the names of some of them, have spent some time in their company through pages that they have shared in other books: Frederick Buechner, Kathleen Norris, Pope Francis, Rowan Williams,

Richard Rohr, Marianne Williamson, Joyce Rupp, Phyllis Tickle, Robert Ellsberg, Anna Quindlen, Brian Doyle, and many others whose homes you have not yet visited but will find warm and inviting and comforting in the pages that follow.

You can read one reflection a day from the first day of Advent through Christmas to the Epiphany or, just as good, you can read one or more any day of the year. That's the beauty of being children of God in this neighborhood where all things are made new. Whenever darkness seems to appear we can always switch on the light. That's what this book is about, and we hope you find it helpful now or any ol' time at all.

Michael Leach, James Keane, Doris Goodnough

Advent

Thomas Merton

Charm with your stainlessness these winter
nights,
Skies, and be perfect! Fly vivider in the fiery dark,
you quiet meteors,
And disappear.
You moon, be slow to go down,
This is your full!

The four white roads make off in silence
Towards the four parts of the starry universe.
Time falls like manna at the corners of the wintry
earth.
We have become more humble than the rocks,

Goodness and Light

More wakeful than the patient hills.
Charm with your stainlessness these nights in
Advent,
holy spheres,
While minds, as meek as beasts,
Stay close at home in the sweet hay;
And intellects are quieter than the flocks that feed
by starlight.

Oh pour your darkness and your brightness over
all our
solemn valleys,
You skies: and travel like the gentle Virgin,
Toward the planets' stately setting,

Oh white full moon as quiet as Bethlehem!

Salvation Army Santa Claus Clangs His Bell

Frederick Buechner

The house lights go off and the footlights come on. Even the chattiest stop chattering as they wait in darkness for the curtain to rise. In the orchestra pit, the violin bows are poised. The conductor has raised his baton.

In the silence of a midwinter dusk there is far off in the deeps of it somewhere a sound so faint that for all you can tell it may be only the sound of the silence itself. You hold your breath to listen.

You walk up the steps to the front door. The empty windows at either side of it tell you nothing, or almost nothing. For a second you catch a whiff in the air of some fragrance that reminds you of a place you've never been and a time you have no words for. You are aware of the beating of your heart.

The extraordinary thing that is about to happen is matched only by the extraordinary moment just before it happens. Advent is the name of that moment.

The Salvation Army Santa Claus clangs his bell. The sidewalks are so crowded you can hardly move. Exhaust fumes are the chief fragrance in the air, and everybody is as bundled up against any sense of what all the fuss is really about as they are bundled up against the windchill factor.

But if you concentrate just for an instant, far off in the deeps of you somewhere you can feel the beating of your heart. For all its madness and lostness, not to mention your own, you can hear the world itself holding its breath.

What Are You Waiting For?

Robert Barron

Advent is the liturgical season of vigilance or, to put it more mundanely, of waiting. During the four weeks prior to Christmas, we light the candles of our Advent wreaths and put ourselves in the spiritual space of the Israelite people who, through many long centuries, waited for the coming of the Messiah ("How long, O Lord?").

In the wonderful avant-garde German movie *Run Lola Run* a young woman finds herself in a terrible bind: She needs to gather an enormous amount of money in a ridiculously short period of time. Throughout the movie she runs and runs, desperately trying through her own frantic efforts to make things right, but nothing works. Finally, at the moment when she finds herself at the absolute limit of her powers, she slows to a trot, looks up to heaven and says, "*Ich warte, ich warte*" (I'm waiting, I'm waiting). Though she does not explicitly address God and though there has been no hint throughout the movie that Lola is the least bit religious, this is undoubtedly a prayer. And in the immediate wake of her edgy request a rather improbable solution to her problem presents itself.

Lola's prayer has always reminded me of Simone Weil, that wonderful and mysterious 20th-century French mystic whose entire spirituality is predicated upon the power of waiting, or—in her language—of expectation. In prayer, Weil taught, we open our souls, expecting God to act even when the content of that expectation remains unclear. In their curious vigilance and hoping against hope, both Lola and Simone are beautiful Advent figures.

Hold Your Horses

Their attitude is, of course, deeply rooted in biblical revelation. From beginning to end of scripture we discover stories of people who are compelled to wait.

The patriarch Abraham received the promise that he would become, despite his old age, the father of a son and through that son the father of descendants more numerous than the stars in the night sky. But the fulfillment of that promise was a long time in coming. Through many years, as he and his wife grew older and older, as the likelihood of their parenthood became increasingly remote, Abraham waited. Did he doubt? Did he wonder whether he had misconstrued the divine promise? Did he waver in his faith? Did he endure the taunts of his enemies and the pitying glances of his friends? Probably. But he waited, and in time the promise came true.

Abraham's great-grandson Joseph, the wearer of the multi-colored coat, saw in a dream that he would be a powerful man and that his brothers would one day bow down to him in homage. But the realization of that dream came only after a long and terrible wait. He was sold into slavery by those very brothers, falsely accused of sexual misconduct, humiliated, and finally sent to prison for seven years. Imagine what it must have been like to endure years in an ancient prison—the discomfort, the total lack of privacy, the terrible food in small amounts, sleeplessness, torture, and above all, hopelessness. This is what Joseph had to wait through before his dream came true in a most unexpected way.

The people of Israel were miraculously delivered from slavery in Egypt, led across the Red Sea by the mighty hand of Moses—and then they waited. A journey that normally would have taken only a few weeks stretched to forty years as they wandered rather aimlessly through the desert. The book of Exodus frequently gives us indications of what this time of vigil was like: "The people grumbled against Moses, 'We are disgusted with this wretched food . . . Why did you lead us out into this desert to die? Were there not graves enough in Egypt?'" (Exodus 16:2-3) They were hardly models of patience.

Even poor Noah had to wait, cooped up in the ark with his irritable family and restless animals while the waters slowly retreated.

In the course of the Christian tradition, there is much evidence of this spirituality of waiting. Relatively late in life Ignatius of Loyola realized he was being called by God to do great things. But before he found his path he passed through a wide variety of experiences in the course of many years: a time of stark asceticism and prayer at Manresa, wandering to the Holy Land and back while living hand-to-mouth and sleeping in doorways, taking elementary courses in Paris alongside young kids, gathering a small band of followers and leading them through the Spiritual Exercises. Only at the end of this long sojourn—founding the Company of Jesus—did he realize the great thing God called him to do.

In Dante's *Purgatorio*, the theme of waiting is on prominent display. Dante and Virgil encounter a number of souls who slouch at the foot of the mountain of Purgatory, destined to make the climb to heaven but compelled for the time being to wait. How long? As long as God determines.

God Has No Express Lane

All of this, I submit, is very hard for most of us. I suppose we human beings have always been in a hurry, but modern people especially seem to want what they want when they want it. We are driven, determined, goal-oriented, fast-moving. I, for one, can't stand waiting.

As a Chicagoan I find myself unavoidably in a lot of traffic jams, and nothing infuriates me more. Usually stuck behind a massive truck, you have no idea when you will get where you want to be, and there is nothing you can do about it.

I hate waiting at doctors' offices; I hate waiting in

9

line at the bank; I hate waiting for the lights to come back on when the electricity fails.

So when I'm told that waiting seems to belong to the heart of the spiritual life, I'm not pleased, for here, too, I want answers, direction, clarity—and I want them pronto. I desire to feel happy and to know what God is up to; I need my life to make sense—now. I'm pleased to live a spiritual life, but I want to be in charge of it and to make it unfold according to my schedule: Run Barron Run. All of this is profoundly antipathetic to the mood and spirit of Advent.

So what sense can we make of the countercultural and counterintuitive spirituality of vigilance? The first thing we have to realize is that we and God are, quite simply, on different time tables. The second letter of Peter states this truth with admirable directness: "To you, O Lord, a thousand years are like a day" (2 Peter 3:8).

To the God who stands outside of space and time and who orders the whole of creation, our hours, days, years, eons have a radically different meaning. What is a long time to us is an instant for God, and hence what seems like delay to us is no delay at all to God. What seems like dumb and pointless waiting to us can be the way that God, in a unique and finally mysterious manner, is working God's purposes out.

Theologian Richard Rohr summed up the spiritual life in the phrase "your life is not about you," and this insight is particularly important in terms of the present question. "Why isn't God acting how I want and when I want?" Perhaps because your life is part of a complex whole, the fullness of which only God can properly grasp and fittingly order.

But we can make things even more specific. Is it possible that we are made to wait because the track we are on is not the one God wants for us? Author G. K. Chesterton said that if you are on the wrong road, the very worst thing you can do is to move quickly. And there is that old joke about the pilot who comes on the intercom and says, "I have good news and bad news, folks: The bad news is that we're totally lost; the good news is that we're making excellent time!" Maybe we're forced to wait because God wants us seriously to reconsider the course we've charted, to stop hurtling down a dangerous road.

Or perhaps we are made to wait because we are not yet adequately prepared to receive what God wants to give us. In his remarkable letter to Proba, Saint Augustine argued that the purpose of unanswered prayer is to force expansion of the heart. When we don't get what we want, we begin to want it more and more, with ever greater insistency, until our souls are on fire with the desire for it. Sometimes it is only a sufficiently expanded and enflamed heart that can take in what God intends to give.

What would happen to us if we received, immediately and on our own terms, everything we wanted? We might be satisfied in a superficial way, but we wouldn't begin to appreciate the preciousness of the gifts. After all, the Israelites had to wait thousands of years before they were ready to receive God's greatest gift.

Even if we are on the right track and even if we desire with sufficient intensity what God wants to give, we still might not be ready to integrate a particular grace into our lives or to handle the implications of it. Joseph the dreamer clearly wanted to be a great man, but if he had been given political power and authority when he was an arrogant kid, the results would have been disastrous both for himself and for those under his control. His many years of suffering—his terrible wait—made him a ruler with both wisdom and deep compassion. And so, when his brothers did indeed finally bow down to him as he foresaw in his dream, he was able to react not in vengeance, but in love: "I am Joseph, your brother."

Three Advent Practices

What practically can we do during the season of waiting and vigil keeping? What are some practices that might incarnate for us the spirituality described here?

How about the classically Catholic discipline of eucharistic adoration? To spend a half-hour or an hour in the presence of the Lord is not to accomplish or achieve very much—it is not really "getting" any-where—but it is a particularly rich form of spiritual waiting.

As you keep vigil before the Blessed Sacrament, bring to Christ some problem or dilemma that you have been fretting over, and then pray Lola's prayer: "Ich warte, ich warte." Say, "Lord, I'm waiting for you to solve this, to show me the way out, the way forward. I've been running, planning, worrying, but now I'm going to let you work." Then, throughout Advent, watch attentively for signs.

Also, when you pray before the Eucharist, allow your desire for the things of God to intensify; allow your heart and soul to expand. Pray, "Lord, make me ready to receive the gifts you want to give," or even, "Lord Jesus, surprise me."

A second—and more offbeat—suggestion: Do a jigsaw puzzle. Find one of those big, complex puzzles with thousands of small pieces, one that requires lots of time and plenty of patience, and make of it an Advent project. As you assemble the puzzle think of each piece as some aspect of your life: a relationship, a loss, a failure, a great joy, an adventure, a place where you lived, something you shouldn't have said, an act of generosity. So often the events of our lives seem like the thousand pieces of a puzzle lying incoherently and disconnectedly before us. As you patiently put the puzzle together meditate on the fact that God is slowly, patiently, according to his own plan and purpose, ordering the seemingly unrelated and incongruous events of our lives into a picture of great beauty.

Finally, take advantage of traffic jams and annoying lines—really anything that makes you wait. And let the truth of what 18th-century spiritual writer Jean-Pierre de Caussade said sink in: "Whatever happens to you in the course of a day, for good or ill, is an expression of God's will." Instead of cursing your luck, banging on the steering wheel, or rolling your eyes in frustration, see the wait as a spiritual invitation.

When you are forced to slow down, pray one of the great, repetitive vigil prayers of the church, such as the rosary or the Jesus prayer ("Lord Jesus Christ, Son of God, have mercy on me, a sinner"). With this resolution in mind, hang a rosary around your rear-view mirror at the beginning of Advent. Consider the possibility that God wants you at that moment to wait and then sanctify the time through one of those savoring prayers.

The entire Bible ends on a note not so much of triumph and completion as longing and expectation: "Come, Lord Jesus." From the very beginning of the Christian dispensation, followers of the risen Jesus have been waiting. Paul, Augustine, Chrysostom, Agnes, Thomas Aquinas, Clare, Francis, John Henry Newman, and Simone Weil have all waited for the Second Coming and have hence all been Advent people. During this season let us join them, turning our eyes and hearts upward and praying, "*Ich warte, ich warte.*"

Christmas Time in Bolivia

Maggie Fogarty

How beautiful upon the mountains are the feet
of the messenger who announces peace, who
brings good news, who announces salvation,
who says to Zion, "Your God reigns."

—Isaiah 52:7

My husband and I and our two young children had been living in Amachuma, Bolivia, for about two years when I had an experience that enabled me to recognize what it truly means to be in mission. It was Christmas time, and a local church had organized a Nativity play for the children in our village. Everyone was thrilled. There would be costumes and hot chocolate and the whole village would be there to watch the play.

On the morning of the play, three little boys came to my door. "Hermana," they said, "we are shepherds in the play, and we need your help for our costumes."

"What do you need?" I asked them.

"We need the towels we've seen drying on your clothes line. We need the big ones for our bodies and the little ones for our heads."

"But Juanito," I said to the oldest boy, "you are already a shepherd. Every single day, after school, you take your family's thirty sheep to pasture, and you wait with them to keep them safe from thieves and hungry dogs. And then you bring them home; you give them food and fresh water; and you put them in their shelter for the night."

And to Carlos I said, "Do you remember one morning last month, when you brought a newborn lamb to my house?" The lamb had been born on a frosty morning, and was freezing to death on the hard ground. Carlos had thought to pick up the lamb, stiff with cold, and run to our house because he had seen us use a portable gas heater in our kitchen. "You saved that little lamb, Carlos. You held it in your arms by our heater until it was warm and kicking to life. That, my friend, makes you a smart and wonderful shepherd."

Now, I don't think my words had much impact on these dear ones in that moment, and they probably wondered why I had tears in my eyes. After all, they were taking their acting roles very seriously and they wanted to look like the shepherds they saw in the pictures of their church's illustrated Bible. And they would feel more appropriately attired in my dish towels and bath towels. So of course, I sent them along, with armloads of towels and a promise that we would be there to take their pictures and applaud for them.

And as we watched the play that night, I knew that if I did nothing else in our time in Bolivia, I would find ways to say to these beautiful children that they are already good enough, that their experiences matter, they know more than they think they know, and they know more than they've been told they know. And they don't need anybody's dish towels to tell a story about God being born in the world.

There were many times during our years in Bolivia that we were given good news to proclaim. We witnessed indigenous people organizing to demand a more just society and a more dignified economy. We witnessed farmers and mothers, miners and teachers insisting, nonviolently, on political change that would honor their values and identity as a nation of indigenous people. When the people of Bolivia elected an Aymara man, a farmer and union leader, as the country's first indigenous president, we said to the children of our Aymara village: "Look, a man who looks like you is now president of your country!"

We read in John: "He himself was not the light, but he came to testify to the light." We missionaries, when we open our eyes and our hearts to the presence of God that surrounds us in the communities where we live, are called to be witnesses to the light that we find there. We proclaim the good news that God is truly among us, in the wisdom and resilience and tenacity of the peoples of the world who have had to fight to stay alive, who are working to reclaim their sacred traditions and language after centuries of conquest, who are trying to create security for themselves and their families in the cruel dynamics of the global economy.

To be in mission is to find a thousand ways to say, "You are beautiful, you are wise and powerful, your ways are wonderful, you are marvelous just as God made you." The good news we proclaim is that those we encounter in mission can show us a path to peace and to our shared salvation.

It is good news for all of us.

✦

Less Is More

Richard Rohr

I have never been busier in my life than I have been recently. What right do I have to talk about contemplation when I have been living on overdrive? It seems that we tend to think that more is better. I am told that busyness is actually a status symbol for us! It is strange that when people have so much, they are so anxious about not having enough—to do, to see, to own, to fix, to control, to change.

Several years ago when I was in Nicaragua, I asked a man if he had time, and he said, "I have the rest of my life," and smiled. Who of us would possibly say that? That is what we don't have. What we don't have is the rest of our lives because we do not even have the now of our lives. The decisions we have made in our past have decided our tomorrows; the credit cards and mortgages, the planned obsolescence of almost everything we own, is keeping us all running. And we are not sure why. We don't have the rest of our lives. They are all determined. They are all assured, insured and worried about ahead of time.

We have grown up with all sorts of time-saving devices, and undoubtedly some of us will receive even more of them at Christmas, perhaps finding under our Christmas trees a waffle maker to save time at breakfast or a bun warmer to make dinner preparation faster. Once we own these devices, then we build bigger kitchens that require more cleaning and more energy to store more of our time-saving devices. All these things will save us time— -not!

Time is exactly what we do not have. What decreases in a culture of affluence is precisely and strangely *time*—along with wisdom and friendship. These are the very things that the human heart was created for, that the human heart feeds on and lives for. No wonder we are producing so many depressed, unhealthy and even violent people, while also leaving a huge carbon footprint on this poor planet.

Jesus said it to us quite clearly: "Why are you so anxious? Why do you run after things like the pagans do? What shall I eat? What shall I wear? You are not to worry about tomorrow. Each day will take care of itself" (Matthew 6:31, 34). But for some reason, mostly what we do is reprocess the past and worry about tomorrow. This must tell us that we have not understood the spiritual message of Jesus very well. Now the very earth is telling us so.

Christmas Is a Sad Season for the Poor

John Cheever

Christmas is a sad season. The phrase came to Charlie an instant after the alarm clock had waked him, and named for him an amorphous depression that had troubled him all the previous evening. The sky outside his window was black. He sat up in bed and pulled the light chain that hung in front of his nose. Christmas is a very sad day of the year, he thought. Of all the millions of people in New York, I am practically the only one who has to get up in the cold black of 6 a.m. on Christmas Day in the morning; I am practically the only one.

He dressed, and when he went downstairs from

the top floor of the rooming house in which he lived, the only sounds he heard were the coarse sounds of sleep; the only lights burning were lights that had been forgotten. Charlie ate some breakfast in an all-night lunchwagon and took an Elevated train uptown. From Third Avenue, he walked over to Park. Park Avenue was dark. House after house put into the shine of the street lights a wall of black windows. Millions and millions were sleeping, and this general loss of consciousness generated an impression of abandonment, as if this were the fall of the city, the end of time. He opened the iron-and-glass doors of the apartment building where he had been working for six months as an elevator operator, and went through the elegant lobby to a locker room at the back. He put on a striped vest with brass buttons, a false ascot, a pair of pants with a light-blue stripe on the seam, and a coat. The night elevator man was dozing on the little bench in the car. Charlie woke him. The night elevator man told him thickly that the day doorman had been taken sick and wouldn't be in that day. With the doorman sick, Charlie wouldn't have any relief for lunch, and a lot of people would expect him to whistle for cabs.

Charlie had been on duty a few minutes when 14

rang—a Mrs. Hewing, who, he happened to know, was kind of immoral. Mrs. Hewing hadn't been to bed yet, and she got into the elevator wearing a long dress under her fur coat. She was followed by her two funny-looking dogs. He took her down and watched her go out into the dark and take her dogs to the curb. She was outside for only a few minutes. Then she came in and he took her up to 14 again. When she got off the elevator, she said, "Merry Christmas, Charlie."

"Well, it isn't much of a holiday for me, Mrs. Hewing," he said. "I think Christmas is a very sad season of the year. It isn't that people around here ain't generous—I mean I got plenty of tips—but, you see, I live alone in a furnished room and I don't have any family or anything, and Christmas isn't much of a holiday for me."

"I'm sorry, Charlie," Mrs. Hewing said. "I don't have any family myself. It is kind of sad when you're alone, isn't it?" She called her dogs and followed them into her apartment. He went down.

It was quiet then, and Charlie lighted a cigarette. The heating plant in the basement encompassed the building at that hour in a regular and profound vibration, and the sullen noises of arriving steam heat began to resound, first in the lobby and then to reverberate up through all the sixteen stories, but this was a mechanical awakening, and it didn't lighten his loneliness or his petulance. The black air outside the glass doors had begun to turn blue, but the blue light seemed to have no source; it appeared in the middle of the air. It was a tearful light, and as it picked out the empty street and the long file of Christmas trees, he wanted to cry. Then a cab drove up, and the Walsers got out, drunk and dressed in evening clothes, and he took them up to their penthouse. The Walsers got him to brooding about the difference between his life in a furnished room and the lives of the people overhead. It was terrible.

Then the early churchgoers began to ring, but there were only three of these that morning. A few more went off to church at eight o'clock, but the majority of the building remained unconscious, although the smell of bacon and coffee had begun to drift into the elevator shaft.

At a little after nine, a nursemaid came down with a child. Both the nursemaid and the child had a deep tan and had just returned, he knew, from Bermuda. He had never been to Bermuda. He, Charlie, was a prisoner, confined eight hours a day to a six-by-eight elevator cage, which was confined, in turn, to a sixteen-story shaft. In one building or another, he had made his living as an elevator operator for ten years. He estimated the average trip at about an eighth of a mile, and when he thought of the thousands of miles he had travelled, when he thought that he might have driven the car through the mists above the Caribbean and set it down on some coral beach in Bermuda, he held the narrowness of his travels against his passengers, as if it were not the nature of the elevator but the pressure of their lives that confined him, as if they had clipped his wings.

He was thinking about this when the DePauls, on 9, rang. They wished him a merry Christmas.

"Well, it's nice of you to think of me," he said as they descended, "but it isn't much of a holiday for me. Christmas is a sad season when you're poor. I live alone in a furnished room. I don't have any family."

"Who do you have dinner with, Charlie?" Mrs. DePaul asked

"I don't have any Christmas dinner," Charlie said. "I just get a sandwich."

"Oh, Charlie!" Mrs. DePaul was a stout woman with an impulsive heart, and Charlie's plaint struck at her holiday mood as if she had been caught in a cloudburst. "I do wish we could share our Christmas dinner with you, you know," she said. "I come from Vermont, you know, and when I was a child, you know, we always used to have a great many people at our table. The mailman, you know, and the school-teacher, and just anybody who didn't have any family of their own, you know, and I wish we could share our dinner with you the way we used to, you know, and I don't see any reason why we can't. We can't have you at the table, you know, because you couldn't leave the elevator—could you?—but just as soon as Mr. De-Paul has carved the goose, I'll give you a ring, and I'll arrange a tray for you, you know, and I want you to come up and at least share our Christmas dinner."

Charlie thanked them, and their generosity surprised him, but he wondered if, with the arrival of friends and relatives, they wouldn't forget their offer.

Then old Mrs. Gadshill rang, and when she wished him a merry Christmas, he hung his head.

"It isn't much of a holiday for me, Mrs. Gadshill," he said. "Christmas is a sad season if you're poor. You see, I don't have any family. I live alone in a furnished room."

"I don't have any family either, Charlie," Mrs. Gadshill said. She spoke with a pointed lack of petulance, but her grace was forced. "That is, I don't have any children with me today. I have three children and seven grandchildren, but none of them can see their way to coming East for Christmas with me. Of course, I understand their problems. I know that it's difficult to travel with children during the holidays, although I always seemed to manage it when I was their age, but people feel differently, and we mustn't condemn them for the things we can't understand. But I know how you feel, Charlie. I haven't any family either. I'm just as lonely as you."

Mrs. Gadshill's speech didn't move him. Maybe she was lonely, but she had a ten-room apartment and three servants and bucks and bucks and diamonds and diamonds, and there were plenty of poor kids in the slums who would be happy at a chance at the food her cook threw away. Then he thought about poor kids. He sat down on a chair in the lobby and thought about them.

They got the worst of it. Beginning in the fall, there was all this excitement about Christmas and how it was a day for them. After Thanksgiving, they couldn't miss it. It was fixed so they couldn't miss it. The wreaths and decorations everywhere, and bells ringing, and trees in the park, and Santa Clauses on every corner, and pictures in the magazines and newspapers and on every wall and window in the city told them that if they were good, they would get what they wanted. Even if they couldn't read, they couldn't miss it. They couldn't miss it even if they were blind. It got into the air the poor kids inhaled. Every time they took a walk, they'd see all the expensive toys in the store windows, and they'd write letters to Santa Claus, and their mothers and fathers would promise to mail them, and after the kids had gone to sleep, they'd burn the letters in the stove. And when it came Christmas morning, how could you explain it, how could you tell them that Santa Claus only visited the rich, that he didn't know about the good? How could you face them when all you had to give them was a balloon or a lollipop?

On the way home from work a few nights earlier, Charlie had seen a woman and a little girl going down Fifty-ninth Street. The little girl was crying. He guessed she was crying, he knew she was crying, because she'd seen all the things in the toy-store windows and couldn't understand why none of them were for her. Her mother did housework, he guessed, or maybe was a waitress, and he saw them going back to a room like his, with green walls and no heat, on Christmas Eve, to eat a can of soup. And he saw the little girl hang up her ragged stocking and fall asleep, and he saw the mother looking through her purse for something to put into the stocking—This reverie was interrupted by a bell on 11. He went up, and Mr. and Mrs. Fuller were waiting. When they wished him a merry Christmas, he said, "Well, it isn't much of a holiday for me, Mrs. Fuller. Christmas is a sad season when you're poor."

"Do you have any children, Charlie?" Mrs. Fuller asked.

"Four living," he said. "Two in the grave." The majesty of his lie overwhelmed him. "Mrs. Leary's a cripple," he added.

"How sad, Charlie," Mrs. Fuller said. She started out of the elevator when it reached the lobby, and then she turned. "I want to give your children some presents, Charlie," she said. "Mr. Fuller and I are going to pay a call now, but when we come back, I want to give you some things for your children."

He thanked her. Then the bell rang on 4, and he went up to get the Westons.

"It isn't much of a holiday for me," he told them when they wished him a merry Christmas. "Christmas is a sad season when you're poor. You see, I live alone in a furnished room."

"Poor Charlie," Mrs. Weston said. "I know just how you feel. During the war, when Mr. Weston was away, I was all alone at Christmas. I didn't have any Christmas dinner or a tree or anything. I just scrambled myself some eggs and sat there and cried." Mr. Weston, who had gone into the lobby, called impatiently to his wife. "I know just how you feel, Charlie," Mrs. Weston said.

By noon, the climate in the elevator shaft had changed from bacon and coffee to poultry and game, and the house, like an enormous and complex homestead, was absorbed in the preparations for a domestic feast. The children and their nursemaids had all returned from the Park. Grandmothers and aunts were arriving in limousines. Most of the people who came through the lobby were carrying packages wrapped in colored paper, and were wearing their best furs and new clothes. Charlie continued to complain to most of the tenants when they wished him a merry Christmas, changing his story from the lonely bachelor to the poor father, and back again, as his mood changed, but this outpouring of melancholy, and the sympathy it aroused, didn't make him feel any better.

At half past one, 9 rang, and when he went up, Mr. DePaul was standing in the door of their apartment holding a cocktail shaker and a glass. "Here's a little Christmas cheer, Charlie," he said, and he poured Charlie a drink. Then a maid appeared with a tray of covered dishes, and Mrs. DePaul came out of the living room. "Merry Christmas, Charlie," she said. "I had Mr. DePaul carve the goose early, so that you could have some, you know. I didn't want to put the dessert on the tray, because I was afraid it would melt, you know, so when we have our dessert, we'll call you."

"And what is Christmas without presents?" Mr. DePaul said, and he brought a large, flat box from the hall and laid it on top of the covered dishes.

"You people make it seem like a real Christmas to me," Charlie said. Tears started into his eyes. "Thank you, thank you."

"Merry Christmas! Merry Christmas!" they called, and they watched him carry his dinner and his present into the elevator. He took the tray and the box into the locker room when he got down. On the tray, there was a soup, some kind of creamed fish, and a serving of goose. The bell rang again, but before he answered it, he tore open the DePauls' box and saw that it held a dressing gown. Their generosity and their cocktail had begun to work on his brain, and he went jubilantly up to 12. Mrs. Gadshill's maid was standing in the door with a tray, and Mrs. Gadshill stood behind her. "Merry Christmas, Charlie!" she said. He thanked her, and tears came into his eyes again. On the way down, he drank off the glass of sherry on Mrs. Gadshill's tray. Mrs. Gadshill's contribution was a mixed grill. He ate the lamb chop with his fingers. The bell was ringing again, and he wiped his face with a paper towel and went up to 11. "Merry Christmas, Charlie," Mrs. Fuller said, and she was standing in the door with her arms full of packages wrapped in silver paper, just like a picture in an advertisement, and Mr. Fuller was beside her with an arm around her, and they both looked as if they were going to cry. "Here are some things I want you to take home to your children," Mrs. Fuller said. "And here's something for Mrs. Leary and here's something for you. And if you want to take these things out to the elevator, we'll have your dinner ready for you in a minute." He carried the things into the elevator and came back for the tray. "Merry Christmas, Charlie!" both of the Fullers called after him as he closed the door. He took their dinner and their presents into the locker room and tore open the box that was marked for him. There was an alligator wallet in it, with Mr.

Fuller's initials in the corner. Their dinner was also goose, and he ate a piece of the meat with his fingers and was washing it down with a cocktail when the bell rang. He went up again. This time it was the Westons. "Merry Christmas, Charlie!" they said, and they gave him a cup of eggnog, a turkey dinner, and a present. Their gift was also a dressing gown. Then 7 rang, and when he went up, there was another dinner and some more toys. Then 14 rang, and when he went up, Mrs. Hewing was standing in the hall, in a kind of negligee, holding a pair of riding boots in one hand and some neckties in the other. She had been crying and drinking. "Merry Christmas, Charlie," she said tenderly. "I wanted to give you something, and I've been thinking about you all morning, and I've been all over the apartment, and these are the only things I could find that a man might want. These are the only things that Mr. Brewer left. I don't suppose you'd have any use for the riding boots, but wouldn't you like the neckties?" Charlie took the neckties and thanked her and hurried back to the car, for the elevator bell had rung three times.

By three o'clock, Charlie had fourteen dinners spread on the table and the floor of the locker room, and the bell kept ringing. Just as he started to eat one, he would have to go up and get another, and he was in the middle of the Parsons' roast beef when he had to go up and get the DePauls' dessert. He kept the door of the locker room closed, for he sensed that the quality of charity is exclusive and that his friends would have been disappointed to find that they were not the only ones to try to lessen his loneliness. There were goose, turkey, chicken, pheasant, grouse, and pigeon. There were trout and salmon, creamed scallops and oysters, lobster, crabmeat, whitebait, and clams. There were plum puddings, mince pies, mousses, puddles of melted ice cream, layer cakes, *Torten, éclairs*, and two slices of Bavarian cream. He had dressing gowns, neckties, cuff links, socks, and handkerchiefs, and one of the tenants had asked for his neck size and then given him three green shirts. There were a glass teapot filled, the label said, with jasmine honey, four bottles of aftershave lotion, some alabaster bookends, and a dozen steak knives. The avalanche of charity he had precipitated filled the locker room and made him hesitant, now and then, as if he had touched some wellspring in the female heart that would bury him alive in food and dressing gowns. He had made almost no headway on the food, for all the servings were preternaturally large, as if loneliness had been counted on to generate in him a brutish appetite. Nor had he opened any of the presents that had been given to him for his imaginary children, but he had drunk everything they sent down, and around him were the dregs of Martinis, Manhattans, Old-Fashioneds, champagne-and-raspberry-shrub cocktails, eggnogs, Bronxes, and Side Cars.

His face was blazing. He loved the world, and the world loved him. When he thought back over his life, it appeared to him in a rich and wonderful light, full of astonishing experiences and unusual friends. He thought that his job as an elevator operator—cruising up and down through hundreds of feet of perilous space—demanded the nerve and the intellect of a birdman. All the constraints of his life—the green walls of his room and the months of unemployment—dissolved. No one was ringing, but he got into the elevator and shot it at full speed up to the penthouse and down again, up and down, to test his wonderful mastery of space.

A bell rang on 12 while he was cruising, and he stopped in his flight long enough to pick up Mrs. Gadshill. As the car started to fall, he took his hands off the controls in a paroxysm of joy and shouted, "Strap on your safety belt, Mrs. Gadshill! We're going to make a loop-the-loop!" Mrs. Gadshill shrieked. Then, for some reason, she sat down on the floor of the elevator. Why was her face so pale, he wondered; why was she sitting on the floor? She shrieked again. He grounded the car gently, and cleverly, he thought, and opened the door. "I'm sorry if I scared you, Mrs. Gadshill," he said meekly. "I was only fooling." She shrieked again. Then she ran out into the lobby, screaming for the superintendent.

The superintendent fired Charlie and took over the elevator himself. The news that he was out of work stung Charlie for a minute. It was his first contact with human meanness that day. He sat down in the locker room and gnawed on a drumstick. His drinks were beginning to let him down, and while it had not reached him yet, he felt a miserable soberness in the offing. The excess of food and presents around him began to make him feel guilty and unworthy. He regretted bitterly the lie he had told about his children. He was a single man with simple needs. He had abused the goodness of the people upstairs. He was unworthy.

Then up through this drunken train of thought

surged the sharp figure of his landlady and her three skinny children. He thought of them sitting in their basement room. The cheer of Christmas had passed them by. This image got him to his feet. The realization that he was in a position to give, that he could bring happiness easily to someone else, sobered him. He took a big burlap sack, which was used for collecting waste, and began to stuff it, first with his presents and then with the presents for his imaginary children. He worked with the haste of a man whose train is approaching the station, for he could hardly wait to see those long faces light up when he came in the door. He changed his clothes, and, fired by a wonderful and unfamiliar sense of power, he slung his bag over his shoulder like a regular Santa Claus, went out the back way, and took a taxi to the lower East Side.

The landlady and her children had just finished off a turkey, which had been sent to them by the local Democratic Club, and they were stuffed and uncomfortable when Charlie began pounding on the door, shouting, "Merry Christmas!" He dragged the bag in after him and dumped the presents for the children onto the floor. There were dolls and musical toys, blocks, sewing kits, an Indian suit, and a loom, and it appeared to him that, as he had hoped, his arrival in the basement dispelled its gloom. When half the presents had been opened, he gave the landlady a bathrobe and went upstairs to look over the things he had been given for himself.

Now, the landlady's children had already received so many presents by the time Charlie arrived that they were confused with receiving, and it was only the landlady's intuitive grasp of the nature of charity that made her allow the children to open some of the presents while Charlie was still in the room, but as soon as he had gone, she stood between the children and the presents that were still unopened. "Now, you kids have had enough already," she said. "You kids have got your share. Just look at the things you got there. Why, you ain't even played with the half of them. Mary Anne, you ain't even looked at that doll the Fire Department give you. Now, a nice thing to do would be to take all this stuff that's left over to those poor people on Hudson Street—them Deckkers. They ain't got nothing." A beatific light came into her face when she realized that she could give, that she could bring cheer, that she could put a healing finger on a case needier than hers, and—like Mrs. DePaul and Mrs. Weston, like Charlie himself and like Mrs. Deckker, when Mrs. Deckker was to think, subsequently, of the poor Shannons—first love, then charity, and then a sense of power drove her. "Now, you kids help me get all this stuff together. Hurry, hurry, hurry," she said, for it was dark then, and she knew that we are bound, one to another, in licentious benevolence for only a single day, and that day was nearly over. She was tired, but she couldn't rest, she couldn't rest.

✳

Christmas to Me

Harper Lee

Several years ago, I was living in New York and working for an airline, so I never got home to Alabama for Christmas—if, indeed, I got the day off. To a displaced Southerner, Christmas in New York can be rather a melancholy occasion, not because the scene is strange to one far from home, but because it is familiar: New York shoppers evince the same singleness of purpose as slow moving Southerners; Salvation Army bands and Christmas carols are alike the world over: at that time of year, New York streets shine wet with the same gentle farmer's rain that soaks Alabama's winter fields.

I missed Christmas away from home, I thought. What I really missed was a memory, an old memory of people long since gone, of my grandparents' house bursting with cousins, smilax, and holly. I missed the sound of hunting boots, the sudden open-door gusts of chilly air that cut through the aroma of pine needles and oyster dressing. I missed my brother's night-before-Christmas mask of rectitude and my father's bumblebee bass humming "Joy to the World."

In New York, I usually spent the day, or what was left of it, with my closest friends in Manhattan. They were a young family in periodically well-to-do circumstances. Periodically, because the head of the household employed the precarious craft of writing for their living. He was brilliant and lively; his one defect of character was an inordinate love of puns. He possessed a trait curious not only in a writer but in a young man with dependents; there was about him a quality of fearless optimism—not of the wishing-makes-it-so variety, but that of seeing an attainable goal and daring to take risks in its pursuit. His audacity sometimes left his friends breathless—who in his circumstances would venture to buy a townhouse in Manhattan? His shrewd generalship made the undertaking successful: while most young people are content to dream of such things, he made his dream a reality for his family and satisfied his tribal longing for his own ground beneath his feet. He had come to New York from the Southwest and, in a manner characteristic of all natives thereof, had found the most beautiful girl in the east and married her.

To this ethereal, utterly feminine creature were born two strapping sons, who, as they grew, discovered that their fragile mother packed a wallop that was second to nobody's. Her capacity to love was enormous, and she spent hours in her kitchen, producing dark, viscous delights for her family and friends.

They were a handsome pair, healthy in mind and body, happy in their extremely active lives. Common interests as well as love drew me to them: an endless flow of reading material circulated amongst us; we took pleasure in the same theatre, films, music; we laughed at the same things, and we laughed so much in those days.

Our Christmases together were simple. We limited our gifts to pennies and wits and all-out competition. Who would come up with the most outrageous for the least? The real Christmas was for the children, an idea I found totally compatible, for I had long ago ceased to speculate on the meaning of Christmas as anything other than a day for children. Christmas to me was only a memory of old loves and empty rooms, something I buried with the past that underwent a vague, aching resurrection every year.

One Christmas, though, was different. I was lucky. I had the whole day off, and I spent Christmas Eve with them. When morning came, I awoke to a small hand kneading my face. "Dup," was all its owner had time to say. I got downstairs just in time to see the little boys' faces as they beheld the pocket rockets and space equipment Santa Claus had left them. At first, their fingers went almost timidly over their toys. When their inspection had been completed, the two boys dragged everything into the center of the living room.

Bedlam prevailed until they discovered there was more. As their father began distributing gifts, I grinned to myself, wondering how my exceptionally wily unearthments this year would be received. His was a print of a portrait of Sydney Smith I'd found for thirty-five cents; hers was the complete works of Margot Asquith, the result of a year's patient search. The children were in agonies of indecision over which package to open next, and as I waited, I noticed that while a small stack of presents mounted beside their mother's chair, I had received not a single one. My disappointment was growing steadily, but I tried not to show it.

They took their time. Finally she said, "We haven't forgotten you. Look on the tree."

There was an envelope on the tree, addressed to me. I opened it and read: "You have one year off from your job to write whatever you please. Merry Christmas."

"What does this mean?" I asked.

"What it says," I was told.

They assured me that it was not some sort of joke. They'd had a good year, they said. They'd saved some money and thought it was high time they did something about me.

"What do you mean, do something about me?"

To tell the truth—if I really wanted to know—they thought I had a great talent, and—

"What makes you think that?"

It was plain to anyone who knew me, they said, if anyone would stop to look. They wanted to show their faith in me the best way they knew how. Whether I ever sold a line was immaterial. They wanted to give me a full, fair chance to learn my craft, free from the harassments of a regular job. Would I accept their gift? There were no strings at all. Please accept, with their love.

It took some time to find my voice. When I did,

I asked if they were out of their minds. What made them think anything would come of this? They didn't have that kind of money to throw away. A year was a long time. What if the children came down with something horrible? As objection crowded upon objection, each was overruled. "We're all young," they said. "We can cope with whatever happens. If disaster strikes, you can always find a job of some kind. Okay, consider it a loan, then, if you wish. We just want you to accept. Just permit us to believe in you. You must."

"It's a fantastic gamble," I murmured. "It's such a great risk."

My friend looked around his living room, at his boys, half buried under a pile of bright Christmas wrapping paper. His eyes sparkled as they met his wife's, and they exchanged a glance of what seemed to me insufferable smugness. Then he looked at me and said softly; "No, honey. It's not a risk. It's a sure thing."

Outside, snow was falling, an odd event for a New York Christmas. I went to the window, stunned by the day's miracle. Christmas trees blurred softly across the street, and firelight made the children's shadows dance on the wall beside me. A full, fair chance for a new life. Not given me by an act of generosity, but by an act of love. Our faith in you was really all I had heard them say. I would do my best not to fail them. Snow still fell on the pavement below. Brownstone roofs gradually whitened. Lights in distant skyscrapers shone with yellow symbols of a road's lonely end, and as I stood at the window, looking at the lights and the snow, the ache of an old memory left me forever.

❦

Magnificat

Joelle Chase

And blessed is she that believed: for there shall be a performance of those things which were told her from the Lord.

And Mary said, My soul doth magnify the Lord,

And my spirit hath rejoiced in God my Saviour.

For he hath regarded the low estate of his hand-maiden:

for, behold, from henceforth all generations shall call me blessed.

For he that is mighty hath done to me great things; and holy is his name.

And his mercy is on them that fear him from generation to generation.

He hath shewed strength with his arm;

he hath scattered the proud in the imagination of their hearts.

He hath put down the mighty from their seats, and exalted them of low degree.

He hath filled the hungry with good things; and the rich he hath sent empty away.

He hath helped his servant Israel, in remembrance of his mercy;

As he spake to our fathers, to Abraham, and to his seed forever.

And Mary abode with [Elizabeth] about three months, and returned to her own house.
—LUKE 1:46-56 KJV

She believed. She remembered. All those Uncle Arthur bedtime stories. Remembered the time God washed Pharaoh's army into the sea. Remembered when God fed the wandering Israelites with manna and quail. Remembered when Nebuchadnezzar nibbled grass like a cow. Remembered when the child Joash became king. Mary remembered God's characteristic blessing and exalting of the humble, and knew it to be true again in her very own self.

It seems to be the clearest pattern in Scripture, particularly in Jesus' life. God is persistently coming to people in slavery, poverty, homelessness, prison, and death, while making foolish and ridiculous the wisdom, strength, and wealth of the upper crust. The mystery of God becoming human through a humble young woman and a baby in a manger is an echo of this truth. Emmanuel—God is with and in our earthy, fully human existence.

Mary is an archetype of the feminine in all of us—man or woman—sometimes hidden or subverted, but always present and available, inviting us to embrace what appears small, unimportant, embarrassing, weak. She knew her strength, the miracle of her body that would knit Life out of God's seed. Richard Rohr writes, "Mary is a woman who is profoundly self-possessed. She can hold her power comfortably because she knows it is from Beyond. She can also give it away. Power, dignity, and blessedness are hers to hold, offer back, and proudly acclaim in her great Magnificat (Luke 1:46-55). This woman knows her boundaries, her ground, and her gift. Her dignity is not earned or attained. It is."

And I believe it is inherent within each of us, regardless of gender—the potential and power for mothering life. Mothers are dangerous, in the way Clarissa Pinkola Estes means. They will stop "at nothing to nourish, protect, and guide." They guard and shelter something that "should not be allowed to pass away from this earth."

Mothers are queens of hospitality, welcoming the runny-nosed, stinky-diapered, whining.

What would it be like for me, for you, to remember this identity? It would go against much of what our culture and religions practice. Identifying with the outcast, acknowledging and even honoring the scary and discomforting parts of our society and selves. Marianne Williamson's well-known celebration of God-breathed humanity, her magnificat, is worth repeating:

> Our deepest fear is not that we are inadequate. Our deepest fear is that we are powerful beyond measure. It is our light, not our darkness that most frightens us. We ask ourselves, Who am I to be brilliant, gorgeous, talented, fabulous? Actually, who are you not

to be? You are a child of God. Your playing small does not serve the world. There is nothing enlightened about shrinking so that other people won't feel insecure around you. We are all meant to shine, as children do. We were born to make manifest the glory of God that is within us. It is not just in some of us; it is in everyone. And as we let our own light shine, we unconsciously give other people permission to do the same. As we are liberated from our own fear, our presence automatically liberates others.

Unwed mothers, undocumented immigrants, homosexuals, prisoners on death row, sweat shop workers. I'm sure you could add to the list of people to "revile." Take a closer look, inward, at the places in you that have been ignored, feared, shunned. It really is these very qualities that God dreams of unleashing, of birthing. But we have to go into the darkness to bring them into the light.

For those of us in the northern hemisphere, Advent is a season of darkness. The days grow shorter. Sure, there are still twenty-four hours in each of them, yet the hours of the sun's gaze are fewer and fewer. We wait longer for sunrise and watch it set earlier every evening. It is the season of death, dormancy and waiting. It is a liminal space in which we light candles to remind us of the luminosity to come.

Descent into darkness is necessary to all life, to transformation and to fresh, new revelations of God. Even in darkness, something is forming. We recite the promise of Messiah's coming, remembering the months of gestation preceding Jesus' birth. We declare, "This is our God—the One who scatters the proud, puts down the mighty, exalts the lowly, fills the hungry, sends the rich away empty, creates beauty and brilliance within our womb, mothers the world with fierce and tender love."

What yet unborn soul-gift in you is waiting to bless the world? And what would it take to nurture it into fullness? How terrifying and empowering would it be to really see the dignity of yourself and everyone else: that all are blessed?

Soda Bread in Tanzania

Sr. Patricia Gallogly, MM

Rejoice always. Pray without ceasing. In all
circumstances give thanks. . . .
— 1 THESSALONIANS 5:16-18A

The soda bread was all the three of us had for breakfast the next morning. I thought, "What should I do?" Esther, our neighbor in the village of Kung'ombe, Tanzania had just brought us water from the spring, a precious gift as our rain barrels had run dry. I had always thought myself generous in sharing with others but at that moment I realized it was always from what I had over and above. Now I was being challenged to give from the little we had. As I cut that bread in half and handed it to Esther, sharing became a new reality for me.

Isaiah speaks today in our first reading about Good News for those who are poor. I knew I was the "poor" here having the Good News preached to me in this event. My eight years living in Kung'ombe was a gift—a learning experience in sharing as a way of life.

How often when I gave a cookie to a child playing in our courtyard, she would immediately break it and share it with her brother. A meal was a shared moment as a family gathered around a common dish. There were no separate bowls or plates for individuals. When I suggested to mothers that it would be good for a small child to have his own bowl to ensure his getting the nourishment needed, I was met with resistance. They feared if the child was not sharing food with others it would result in him becoming greedy. There was no place for a greedy person in village life.

In recent years we've all been awakened to the fact that the economic and many of the social problems we are facing as a people have their roots in greed. Conspicuous consumption is all around us. The more we have the happier we'll be, we think. But of course we never have enough. So it just becomes more and more and more.

Again, living a life of sharing tells me I am never alone. I depend on my neighbor and my neighbor depends on me. We wait for the rains knowing without them there'll be no harvest. Hunger would be our lot. But today we are together and we have what we need for right now. We sit chatting, laughing and singing as we prepare the maize for the evening meal. Yes, there's always laughter. Why not, we are alive and God is caring for us.

And so St. Paul tells us today to be happy—Rejoice! How privileged I was to live with people who knew how to rejoice. They had not been touched by consumerism. Their preparation for Christmas centered on the reason for this feast.

How often I've shared the experiences of my life in Tanzania with friends and family here in the U.S. There's interest but somehow the core of the message was always missed. Rejoicing in the day . . . the moment with no surety about tomorrow could not really be comprehended.

"A voice in the wilderness" is what John the Baptist calls himself in today's Gospel. Somehow this message of sharing and living in communion with one another may seem to be lost in the wilderness. We are surrounded by consumerism and greed as people desire to accumulate more riches.

The "recycle" image is a familiar one for all of us.

We see it on the bottom of plastic bottles and as a logo on shopping bags. At times we'll see the words "Reduce, Reuse, Recycle" on each of the arrows. But I wonder how often we pay attention to it. "A voice in the wilderness," its message is in total contrast to the consumer message.

As we continue our Advent journey let us hold this symbol before us—a reminder we are one community, sharing our bread with one another. Together we can "make straight the way of the Lord" by walking hand in hand gently upon our beautiful planet, Earth.

⤜⤙

The Time Machine

Anna Quindlen

Once upon a time there was a dollhouse. Santa brought it via UPS. The dollhouse was enormous, and when push came to shove—well, neither made any difference. It wouldn't fit in the car for the trip out to the country. Comet and Cupid were busy, so Mom called Pick-up—that is, the little girl's grandfather, who owned one. The dollhouse got to where it was going, which was under the tree, and all was right with the world. If you don't believe it, check out the home movies. The little girl looks down from the top of the stairs and her Raggedy Ann eyes are on high beam. "A dollhouse," she croons. It was all worth it.

Was it all worth it? Whatever happened to that dollhouse? Younger cousin? Garage sale? Beats me.

And yet it seemed so incredibly important at the time, the time being this time, when being Santa morphs into being beleaguered. That isn't new. In 1874 a British actress named Fanny Kemble wrote "Christmas is a season of such infinite labour, as well as expense in the shopping and present-making line, that almost every woman I know is good for nothing in purse and person for a month afterwards."

Finally, the much-vaunted war against Christmas, dreamed up by conservative megaphoners to decry irreligious department-store advertisements and town-square displays, seems to have run its course, toppled by its sheer irrelevance. But the worst thing about it was that it disguised the true war on the season, which takes place at home. I know; I'm a former foot soldier.

Power Rangers, Cabbage Patch dolls, mutant turtles. So many items made of plastic that needed to be tracked down and swiftly snagged. Surely, Mary and Joseph can't have trekked to Bethlehem, Herod and the Magi in hot pursuit, so that modern pilgrims could track down the trendiest toys. But since Santa brought what was requested by good little boys and girls, the absence of desired items beneath the tree could only be explained by two unthinkable eventualities: kids not good, or Santa not real. It was hard to get around that. Suffice it to say that Toys "R" Us is the only retail establishment I have ever visited at dawn.

There's a bromide about this: don't sweat the small stuff, and it's all small stuff. That's absurd. Lots of small stuff is really big. My children can track their childhoods in tree ornaments: the china bell for Baby's first Christmas, the triangle of felt and photograph made in Miss Hawe's third-grade class, the dinosaurs that marked the passionate enthusiasm of the onetime natural historian. The essence of the season lies in figuring out what small stuff is passing minutiae and what is enduring memory. Come to think of it, that may well be the essence of everything.

In another Christmas home movie, the former dino boy, then aged five, looks into the lens and says as though he is imparting a great secret, "Do you know what a camera is? It's a time machine." I wish I had a time machine, if only so my older self could speak for just a few seconds to my younger one, to tell her to chill: everyone will survive if Talking Big Bird is sold out. It was only recently, many years after the event, that I discovered that little boy giving me the time-machine tip, a ghost of Christmas past. What trivial pursuit made me miss it at the time? Thank God the VCR offered me a second chance.

There's a story my father likes to tell about a Christmas many years ago, when the Depression meant that Santa's sack was slack. Late on Christmas Eve my grandfather, who had many children but no tree, drove up to the post office, where a fresh-cut fir had been placed over the lintel. He parked against the post office door and climbed on the car roof, at which point a police cruiser approached. When my grandfather told the officer what he was trying to do, the cop helped him take the tree down and put it in the car.

Everyone involved in this story is Irish, so I'm willing to accept that it may be apocryphal, but I don't care. It's about the spirit of Christmas because it's about understanding the power of the small symbol. As it says in "A Christmas Carol" about the Cratchits' pudding, "Everybody had something to say about it, but nobody said or thought it was at all a small pudding for a large family. It would have been flat heresy to do so."

The most enduring tales about Christmas are about recapturing those small moments, Scrooge and George Bailey on a guided tour of their own wonderful lives. But you don't really need the help of ghosts and angels. The truth is that once you've watched kids on a Christmas-morning high of ripping packages open, gloating over the contents for a nanosecond, and then moving thoughtlessly on to the next thing, you know that's not what they will ever take away from the day. You understand the power of that uncommon humdrum thing that glows in memory. That's what I would tell my younger self if I could go back. Find that. Worry about that. Make sure they have that.

The spirit of Christmas is a time machine.

Everything else is just plastic.

~~~

Mary Christ Bus

Brian Doyle

Most of all I remember scents and smells and redo-
lences: pies of various savors and size, glorious new
basketballs, smoke wriggling from the fireplace
where birch and beech and pencils and young squirrels and once a baseball cap all burned fitfully; and
the grandfatherly smell of wet rubber boots steaming
on sprawled newspapers by the door, and the dense
brown cigar-and-sweater scent of uncles avunculat-
ing in their chairs, and the murky cinnamon sea of
egg-nog; and there were seas of sound, too, the radio
faintly yammering the Knick game, and the snicker-
ing of cousins, and the snarling of clan elders not at all
averse to pinning the fingers of children snatching for
a slab of turkey before they, the elders, have fully dis-

membered said vast and mountainous bird, my brothers and I all have knife scars from clan elders who were almighty quick with the blade, being of ancient lines of warriors and knowing full well what they were about weapon-wise; and the roaring of the father downstairs where he is fixing yet another god-blasted storm window smashed by his sons as wild as wolves, and the slim rustling prayer of the mother sliding gracefully through each scene beaming like an actress, and the bark of a brother barfing in the back yard because he won a bet by eating twenty snickerdoodles made by our cousin the nun and he, the brother, did not think this would affect him overmuch but o it did o god did it o god that is hilarious look at the colors, which thank god for a heavy snowfall is all I can say.

The afternoon shuffled along like a quiet country road, and I dozed by the fire, buttocks facing the roasting squirrels and pencils, and in the evening we listened to that preening genius Bishop Fulton Sheen chanting Mass on the radio, and no one knew where the paper plates were at all one bit, and someone snuck a beer from a sleeping uncle whose grip was poor, and someone female and mature read Dylan Thomas aloud, trying unsuccessfully for his cracked drunken Welsh lilt, and there were so many pies you could not choose among them but sat stunned amid mounds of mince, until a grandmother, tart and Irish and smelling of stern and unforgiving soap, gave you such a vast slab of each that your plate looked very much like a whole pie its own self.

Sometimes then we were allowed to open a few presents, just because, although the Great Unraveling was always in the morning, and once I remember opening a present on which a very young niece had written **MARY CHRIST BUS** with all her might, with every iota of her tongue-clenched diligence, and if I was a wise man, which I am not, I would have saved that scrap of extraordinary American literature, and folded it into my battered wallet, so that I could even now, a thousand years later, pull it out ever so gently, and open it up with the utmost care, and see the world as it is, ancient and glorious and fragile and timeless, and written endlessly by the young.

And so then finally to bed.

⤜

The Burglar's Christmas

Willa Cather

Two very shabby looking young men stood at the corner of Prairie avenue and Eightieth street, looking despondently at the carriages that whirled by. It was Christmas Eve, and the streets were full of vehicles; florists' wagons, grocers' carts and carriages. The streets were in that half-liquid, half congealed condition peculiar to the streets of Chicago at that season of the year. The swift wheels that spun by sometimes threw the slush of mud and snow over the two young men who were talking on the corner.

"Well," remarked the elder of the two, "I guess we are at our rope's end, sure enough. How do you feel?"

"Pretty shaky. The wind's sharp tonight. If I had

had anything to eat I mightn't mind it so much. There is simply no show. I'm sick of the whole business. Looks like there's nothing for it but the lake."

"O, nonsense, I thought you had more grit. Got anything left you can hoc?"

"Nothing but my beard, and I am afraid they wouldn't find it worth a pawn ticket," said the younger man ruefully, rubbing the week's growth of stubble on his face.

"Got any folks anywhere? Now's your time to strike 'em if you have."

"Never mind if I have, they're out of the question."

"Well, you'll be out of it before many hours if you don't make a move of some sort. A man's got to eat. See here, I am going down to Longtin's saloon. I used to play the banjo in there with a couple of coons, and I'll bone him for some of his free lunch stuff. You'd better come along, perhaps they'll fill an order for two."

"How far down is it?"

"Well, it's clear down town, of course, way down on Michigan avenue."

"Thanks, I guess I'll loaf around here. I don't feel equal to the walk, and the cars—well, the cars are crowded." His features drew themselves into what might have been a smile under happier circumstances.

"No, you never did like street cars, you're too aristocratic. See here, Crawford, I don't like leaving you here. You ain't good company for yourself tonight."

"Crawford? O, yes, that's the last one. There have been so many I forget them."

"Have you got a real name, anyway?"

"O, yes, but it's one of the ones I've forgotten. Don't you worry about me. You go along and get your free lunch. I think I had a row in Longtin's place once. I'd better not show myself there again." As he spoke the young man nodded and turned slowly up the avenue.

He was miserable enough to want to be quite alone. Even the crowd that jostled by him annoyed him. He wanted to think about himself. He had avoided this final reckoning with himself for a year now. He had laughed it off and drunk it off. But now, when all those artificial devices which are employed to turn our thoughts into other channels and shield us from ourselves had failed him, it must come. Hunger is a powerful incentive to introspection.

It is a tragic hour, that hour when we are finally driven to reckon with ourselves, when every avenue of mental distraction has been cut off and our own life and all its ineffaceable failures closes about us like the walls of that old torture chamber of the Inquisition. Tonight, as this man stood stranded in the streets of the city, his hour came. It was not the first time he had been hungry and desperate and alone. But always before there had been some outlook, some chance ahead, some pleasure yet untasted that seemed worth the effort, some face that he fancied was, or would be, dear. But it was not so tonight. The unyielding conviction was upon him that he had failed in everything, had outlived everything. It had been near him for a long time, that Pale Spectre. He had caught its shadow at the bottom of his glass many a time, at the head of his bed when he was sleepless at night, in the twilight shadows when some great sunset broke upon him. It had made life hateful to him when he awoke in the morning before now. But now it settled slowly over him, like night, the endless Northern nights that bid the sun a long farewell. It rose up before him like granite. From this brilliant city with its glad bustle of Yuletide he was shut off as completely as though he were a creature of another species. His days seemed numbered and done, sealed over like the little coral cells at the bottom of the sea. Involuntarily he drew that cold air through his lungs slowly, as though he were tasting it for the last time.

Yet he was but four and twenty, this man—he looked even younger—and he had a father some place down East who had been very proud of him once. Well, he had taken his life into his own hands, and this was what he had made of it. That was all there was to be said. He could remember the hopeful things they used to say about him at college in the old days, before he had cut away and begun to live by his wits, and he found courage to smile at them now. They had read him wrongly. He knew now that he never had the essentials of success, only the superficial agility that is often mistaken for it. He was tow without the tinder, and he had burnt himself out at other people's fires. He had helped other people to make it win, but he himself—he had never touched an enterprise that had not failed eventually. Or, if it survived his connection with it, it left him behind.

His last venture had been with some ten-cent specialty company, a little lower than all the others, that had gone to pieces in Buffalo, and he had worked his way to Chicago by boat. When the boat made up its crew for the outward voyage, he was dispensed with as usual. He was used to that. The reason for it? O, there are so many reasons for failure! His was a very common one.

As he stood there in the wet under the street light he drew up his reckoning with the world and decided that it had treated him as well as he deserved. He had overdrawn his account once too often. There had been a day when he thought otherwise; when he had said he was unjustly handled, that his failure was merely the lack of proper adjustment between himself and other men, that some day he would be recognized and it would all come right. But he knew better than that now, and he was still man enough to bear no grudge against any one—man or woman.

Tonight was his birthday, too. There seemed something particularly amusing in that. He turned up a limp little coat collar to try to keep a little of the wet chill from his throat, and instinctively began to remember all the birthday parties he used to have. He was so cold and empty that his mind seemed unable to grapple with any serious question. He kept thinking about ginger bread and frosted cakes like a child. He could remember the splendid birthday parties his mother used to give him, when all the other little boys in the block came in their Sunday clothes and creaking shoes, with their ears still red from their mother's towel, and the pink and white birthday cake, and the stuffed olives and all the dishes of which he had been particularly fond, and how he would eat and eat and then go to bed and dream of Santa Claus. And in the morning he would awaken and eat again, until by night the family doctor arrived with his castor oil, and poor William used to dolefully say that it was altogether too much to have your birthday and Christmas all at once. He could remember, too, the royal birthday suppers he had given at college, and the stag dinners, and the toasts, and the music, and the good fellows who had wished him happiness and really meant what they said.

And since then there were other birthday suppers that he could not remember so clearly; the memory of them was heavy and flat, like cigarette smoke that has been shut in a room all night, like champagne that has been a day opened, a song that has been too often sung, an acute sensation that has been overstrained. They seemed tawdry and garish, discordant to him now. He rather wished he could forget them altogether.

Whichever way his mind now turned there was one thought that it could not escape, and that was the idea of food. He caught the scent of a cigar suddenly, and felt a sharp pain in the pit of his abdomen and a sudden moisture in his mouth. His cold hands clenched angrily, and for a moment he felt that bitter hatred of wealth, of ease, of everything that is well-fed and well-housed that is common to starving men. At any rate he had a right to eat! He had demanded great things from the world once: fame and wealth and admiration. Now it was simply bread—and he would have it! He looked about him quickly and felt the blood begin to stir in his veins. In all his straits he had never stolen anything, his tastes were above it. But tonight there would be no tomorrow. He was amused at the way in which the idea excited him. Was it possible there was yet one more experience that would distract him, one thing that had power to excite his jaded interest? Good! he had failed at everything else, now he would see what his chances would be as a common thief. It would be amusing to watch the beautiful consistency of his destiny work itself out even in that role. It would be interesting to add another study to his gallery of futile attempts, and then label them all: "the failure as a journalist," "the failure as a lecturer," "the failure as a business man," "the failure as a thief," and so on, like the titles under the pictures of the Dance of Death. It was time that Childe Roland came to the dark tower.

A girl hastened by him with her arms full of packages. She walked quickly and nervously, keeping well within the shadow, as if she were not accustomed to carrying bundles and did not care to meet any of her friends. As she crossed the muddy street, she made an effort to lift her skirt a little, and as she did so one of the packages slipped unnoticed from beneath her arm. He caught it up and overtook her. "Excuse me, but I think you dropped something."

She started, "O, yes, thank you, I would rather have lost anything than that."

The young man turned angrily upon himself. The package must have contained something of value. Why had he not kept it? Was this the sort of thief he would make? He ground his teeth together. There is nothing more maddening than to have morally consented to crime and then lack the nerve force to carry it out.

A carriage drove up to the house before which he stood. Several richly dressed women alighted and went in. It was a new house, and must have been built since he was in Chicago last. The front door was open and he could see down the hallway and up the stair case. The servant had left the door and gone with the guests. The first floor was brilliantly lighted, but the windows upstairs were dark. It looked very easy, just to slip upstairs to the darkened chambers where the jewels and trinkets of the fashionable occupants were kept.

Still burning with impatience against himself he entered quickly. Instinctively he removed his mud-stained hat as he passed quickly and quietly up the stair case. It struck him as being a rather superfluous courtesy in a burglar, but he had done it before he had thought. His way was clear enough, he met no one on the stairway or in the upper hall. The gas was lit in the upper hall. He passed the first chamber door through sheer cowardice. The second he entered quickly, thinking of something else lest his courage should fail him, and closed the door behind him. The light from the hall shone into the room through the transom. The apartment was furnished richly enough to justify his expectations. He went at once to the dressing case. A number of rings and small trinkets lay in a silver tray. These he put hastily in his pocket. He opened the upper drawer and found, as he expected, several leather cases. In the first he opened was a lady's watch, in the second a pair of old-fashioned bracelets; he seemed to dimly remember having seen bracelets like them before, somewhere. The third case was heavier, the spring was much worn, and it opened easily. It held a cup of some kind. He held it up to the light and then his strained nerves gave way and he uttered a sharp exclamation. It was the silver mug he used to drink from when he was a little boy.

The door opened, and a woman stood in the doorway facing him. She was a tall woman, with white hair, in evening dress. The light from the hall streamed in upon him, but she was not afraid. She stood looking at him a moment, then she threw out her hand and went quickly toward him.

"Willie, Willie! Is it you!"

He struggled to loose her arms from him, to keep her lips from his cheek. "Mother—you must not! You do not understand! O, my God, this is worst of all!" Hunger, weakness, cold, shame, all came back to him, and shook his self-control completely. Physically he was too weak to stand a shock like this. Why could it not have been an ordinary discovery, arrest, the station house and all the rest of it. Anything but this! A hard dry sob broke from him. Again he strove to disengage himself.

"Who is it says I shall not kiss my son? O, my boy, we have waited so long for this! You have been so long in coming, even I almost gave you up."

Her lips upon his cheek burnt him like fire. He put

his hand to his throat, and spoke thickly and incoherently: "You do not understand. I did not know you were here. I came here to rob—it is the first time—I swear it—but I am a common thief. My pockets are full of your jewels now. Can't you hear me? I am a common thief!"

"Hush, my boy, those are ugly words. How could you rob your own house? How could you take what is your own? They are all yours, my son, as wholly yours as my great love—and you can't doubt that, Will, do you?"

That soft voice, the warmth and fragrance of her person stole through his chill, empty veins like a gentle stimulant. He felt as though all his strength were leaving him and even consciousness. He held fast to her and bowed his head on her strong shoulder, and groaned aloud.

"O, mother, life is hard, hard!"

She said nothing, but held him closer. And O, the strength of those white arms that held him! O, the assurance of safety in that warm bosom that rose and fell under his cheek! For a moment they stood so, silently. Then they heard a heavy step upon the stair. She led him to a chair and went out and closed the door. At the top of the staircase she met a tall, broad-shouldered man, with iron gray hair, and a face alert and stern. Her eyes were shining and her cheeks on fire, her whole face was one expression of intense determination.

"James, it is William in there, come home. You must keep him at any cost. If he goes this time, I go with him. O, James, be easy with him, he has suffered so." She broke from a command to an entreaty, and laid her hand on his shoulder. He looked questioningly at her a moment, then went in the room and quietly shut the door.

She stood leaning against the wall, clasping her temples with her hands and listening to the low indistinct sound of the voices within. Her own lips moved silently. She waited a long time, scarcely breathing. At last the door opened, and her husband came out. He stopped to say in a shaken voice,

"You go to him now, he will stay. I will go to my room. I will see him again in the morning."

She put her arm about his neck, "O, James, I thank you, I thank you! This is the night he came so long ago, you remember? I gave him to you then, and now you give him back to me!"

"Don't, Helen," he muttered. "He is my son, I have never forgotten that. I failed with him. I don't like to fail, it cuts my pride. Take him and make a man of him." He passed on down the hall.

She flew into the room where the young man sat with his head bowed upon his knee. She dropped upon her knees beside him. Ah, it was so good to him to feel those arms again!

"He is so glad, Willie, so glad! He may not show it, but he is as happy as I. He never was demonstrative with either of us, you know."

"O, my God, he was good enough," groaned the man. "I told him everything, and he was good enough. I don't see how either of you can look at me, speak to me, touch me." He shivered under her clasp again as when she had first touched him, and tried weakly to throw her off.

But she whispered softly,

"This is my right, my son."

Presently, when he was calmer, she rose. "Now, come with me into the library, and I will have your dinner brought there."

As they went down stairs she remarked apologetically, "I will not call Ellen tonight; she has a number of guests to attend to. She is a big girl now, you know, and came out last winter. Besides, I want you all to myself tonight."

When the dinner came, and it came very soon, he fell upon it savagely. As he ate she told him all that had transpired during the years of his absence, and how his father's business had brought them there. "I was glad when we came. I thought you would drift West. I seemed a good deal nearer to you here."

There was a gentle unobtrusive sadness in her tone that was too soft for a reproach.

"Have you everything you want? It is a comfort to see you eat."

He smiled grimly, "It is certainly a comfort to me. I have not indulged in this frivolous habit for some thirty-five hours."

She caught his hand and pressed it sharply, uttering a quick remonstrance.

"Don't say that! I know, but I can't hear you say it,—it's too terrible! My boy, food has choked me many a time when I have thought of the possibility of that. Now take the old lounging chair by the fire, and if you are too tired to talk, we will just sit and rest together."

He sank into the depths of the big leather chair with the lion's heads on the arms, where he had sat so often in the days when his feet did not touch the floor and he was half afraid of the grim monsters cut in the polished wood. That chair seemed to speak to him of things long forgotten. It was like the touch of an old familiar friend. He felt a sudden yearning tenderness for the happy little boy who had sat there and dreamed of the big world so long ago. Alas, he had been dead many a summer, that little boy!

He sat looking up at the magnificent woman beside him. He had almost forgotten how handsome she was; how lustrous and sad were the eyes that were set under that serene brow, how impetuous and wayward the mouth even now, how superb the white throat and shoulders! Ah, the wit and grace and fineness of this woman! He remembered how proud he had been of her as a boy when she came to see him at school. Then in the deep red coals of the grate he saw the faces of other women who had come since then into his vexed, disordered life. Laughing faces, with eyes artificially bright, eyes without depth or meaning, features without the stamp of high sensibilities. And he had left this face for such as those!

He sighed restlessly and laid his hand on hers. There seemed refuge and protection in the touch of her, as in the old days when he was afraid of the dark. He had been in the dark so long now, his confidence was so thoroughly shaken, and he was bitterly afraid of the night and of himself.

"Ah, mother, you make other things seem so false. You must feel that I owe you an explanation, but I can't make any, even to myself. Ah, but we make poor exchanges in life. I can't make out the riddle of it all. Yet there are things I ought to tell you before I accept your confidence like this."

"I'd rather you wouldn't, Will. Listen: Between you and me there can be no secrets. We are more alike than other people. Dear boy, I know all about it. I am a woman, and circumstances were different with me, but we are of one blood. I have lived all your life before you. You have never had an impulse that I have not known, you have never touched a brink that my feet have not trod. This is your birthday night. Twenty-four years ago I foresaw all this. I was a young woman then and I had hot battles of my own, and I felt your likeness to me. You were not like other babies. From the hour you were born you were restless and discontented, as I had been before you. You used to brace your strong little limbs against mine and try to throw me off as you did tonight. Tonight you have come back to me, just as you always did after you ran away to swim in the river that was forbidden you, the river you loved because it was forbidden. You are tired and sleepy, just as you used to be then, only a little older and a little paler and a little more foolish. I never asked you where you had been then, nor will I now. You have come back to me, that's all in all to me. I know your every possibility and limitation, as a composer knows his instrument."

He found no answer that was worthy to give to talk like this. He had not found life easy since he had lived by his wits. He had come to know poverty at close quarters. He had known what it was to be gay with an empty pocket, to wear violets in his button hole when he had not breakfasted, and all the hateful shams of the poverty of idleness. He had been a reporter on a big metropolitan daily, where men grind out their brains on paper until they have not one idea left—and still grind on. He had worked in a real estate office, where ignorant men were swindled. He had sung in a comic opera chorus and played Harris in an Uncle Tom's Cabin Company, and edited a Socialist weekly. He had been dogged by debt and hunger and grinding poverty, until to sit here by a warm fire without concern as to how it would be paid for seemed unnatural.

He looked up at her questioningly. "I wonder if you know how much you pardon?"

"O, my poor boy, much or little, what does it matter? Have you wandered so far and paid such a bitter price for knowledge and not yet learned that love has nothing to do with pardon or forgiveness, that it only loves, and loves—and loves? They have not taught you well, the women of your world." She leaned over and kissed him, as no woman had kissed him since he left her.

He drew a long sigh of rich content. The old life, with all its bitterness and useless antagonism and flimsy sophistries, its brief delights that were always tinged with fear and distrust and unfaith, that whole miserable, futile, swindled world of Bohemia seemed immeasurably distant and far away, like a dream that is over and done. And as the chimes rang joyfully outside and sleep pressed heavily upon his eyelids, he wondered dimly if the Author of this sad little riddle of ours were not able to solve it after all, and if the Potter would not finally mete out his all comprehensive justice, such as none but he could have, to his Things of Clay, which are made in his own patterns, weak or strong, for his own ends; and if some day we will not awaken and find that all evil is a dream, a mental distortion that will pass when the dawn shall break.

The Smell of Sheep

Carlo Carretto

During advent I found myself in the pale hot hills of Béni-Abbès, that fantastic oasis in the Sahara. I wanted to prepare myself for Christmas in solitude, and the place I had chosen was Ouarourout, where water was abundant and a small natural cave could serve as a chapel. I set out after the feast of the Immaculate Conception (December 8) in wonderful weather and with a great longing to be alone. But the weather soon changed and the desert became cold and gray due to the high mist that covered the sun. And even my solitude was not what I expected, for soon I was discovered by Ali, son of Mohamed Assani.

Ali was a good friend who brought his eleven sheep to graze round about and was thirsting for company and conversation. He assured me that he couldn't find better or richer pastures for his flock than near the well of Ouarourout. He kept his distance, of course, because he knew that when I was praying he had to keep away and not disturb me. But the well was common property so naturally he took the opportunity of coming near when I went to draw water, and then he profited by the occasion to invite me to tea—having taken all the necessaries from my tent.

Ali made tea very well, and he loved drinking it with me; he also liked my bread, which I baked under the ashes. Then off he went to the pastures and for the whole day contented himself with keeping his eye on me from a distance while he searched the sand for little fossils and archeological remains such as tips of arrows from the stone age, which he could then come and sell to me.

The weather grew worse and I had to reinforce my tent ropes against the windstorm which would surely follow. Windstorms in the desert are appalling, developing as they do into sandstorms, and anyone who has been in the desert knows what a sandstorm is like To describe the sort of thing that can happen, suffice it to say that even at midday you have to switch on the headlights of the van if you want to see the track, and the windows and the paintwork are nearly worn away by the violence of the sand.

My one refuge was my cave, and, when the storm came, there I decided to stay night and day so as not to interrupt my retreat. As for Ali, I had not seen him for a day or two so I told myself that he must have foreseen the storm and prudently returned to the fold and his father's tent situated about eight miles from Ouarourout, at the intersection with the road to Bechar.

Not a bit of it!

There I was praying in my cave when he came rushing in, crook in hand and wild with worry. "Come quickly, Brother Carlo, come and help me. My sheep are lost, they're dying in the sand."

I dashed to the van and together we plunged into the desert, a desert furious with blinding wind and sand. It wasn't easy to find the sheep in that inferno. They were frightened and enfeebled and wandering helplessly in the gusts of sand and rain which had now started to fall. I have never seen anything like it. Once again I realized how narrow is the line between life and death in the desert.

While I was at the steering wheel and trying not

to get lost, Ali was pouncing on his sheep and pil-
ing them one by one into the van—they were weak
with exhaustion and numb with fear. Somehow we
managed to get them into my cave, the only possible
refuge from the breathtaking hurricane. So my little
cave was full of wooliness, of bleating, and of the acrid
smell of sheep. I was reminded of the cave at Bethlehem, and I tried to get warm by snuggling up against
the largest sheep—they were as drenched as I was and
shivering in the evening dusk.

I took the Eucharist from the tabernacle and hung
the pyx round my neck under my cloak.

Naturally we did not manage to light the fire for
supper, so we had to be satisfied with eating bread and
a tin of sardines. But Ali liked the sardines.

For myself, I wanted to pray, and I soon realized
that things hadn't gone too badly for me in the tur-
moil of the storm. Wasn't I living through a very special night? It was near to Christmas. I was in a cave
with a shepherd. I was cold. There were sheep and the
stench of dung. Nothing was missing.

The Eucharist that I had hung round my neck
made me think of Jesus present there under the sign
of bread, so like the sign of Bethlehem, the land of
bread. The night advanced. Outside the storm con-

tinued to rage over the desert. Now all was silence in the cave. The sheep filled up the available space. Ali slept curled in his cloak with his head resting on the back of a sheep and with two lambs at his feet. Meanwhile I prayed, reciting Luke's Gospel from memory:

> And while they were there, the time came for her to be delivered. And she gave birth to her first-born son and wrapped him in swaddling cloths, and laid him in a manger, because there was no place for them in the inn (Luke 2:6).

Then I was silent and waited.

Mary became my prayer and I felt her to be very, very close to me. Jesus was in the Eucharist just there under my cloak. All my faith, all my hope, all my love were united in one point. I had no need to meditate; I only had to contemplate in silence. The whole night was at my disposal and dawn was still far off.

Advent Is about Desire

James Martin, SJ

"Advent is all about desire," an elderly Jesuit in our community used to say every year as November drew to a close. And whenever he said it, I would say, "Huh?"

But gradually it dawned on me. Christians desire the coming of Christ into their lives in new ways, a desire that is heightened during Advent. The beautiful readings from the Book of Isaiah, which we hear during Advent, describe how even the earth longs for the presence of God. The wonderful "O antiphons," sung at evening prayer and during the Gospel acclamations towards the end of Advent, speak of Christ as the "King of Nations and their Desire." The Gospel readings in the coming weeks tell of John the Baptist expressing Israel's hope for a Messiah. Mary and Joseph look forward to the upcoming birth of a son. My friend was right. It's all about desire.

But there's a problem: desire has a bad rep in some religious circles. When some of us hear the term they think of two things: sexual desire or material wants, both of which are condemned outright by some shortsighted religious leaders. The first is one of the greatest gifts from God to humanity; without it the human race would cease to exist. The second is part of our natural desire for a healthy life—for food, shelter and clothing.

Desire may also be difficult for some people to accept in their spiritual lives. One of my favorite books on Ignatian spirituality is *The Spiritual Exercises Reclaimed*, written by Katherine Dyckman, Mary Garvin and Elizabeth Liebert, three women religious. In his classic text, *The Spiritual Exercises*, St. Ignatius Loyola repeatedly recommends praying for what "I want and desire." For example, a closer relationship with God. Or a particular grace during a meditation period. The three authors astutely note that this dynamic may present obstacles for some women. "Women may often feel that paying attention to their desires is somehow selfish and that they should not honor their desires if they are being truly generous with God." The authors strongly encourage women to resist that tendency and to "notice" and "name" their desires. To claim them as their own.

Why all this emphasis on desire? Because desire is a key way that God speaks to us, whether in Advent or the rest of the year. Our holy desires are gifts from God.

Holy desires are different than surface wants, like "I want a new smartphone" or "I want a bigger office." Instead I'm talking about our deepest longings, those that shape our lives: desires that help us know who we are to become and what we are to do. Our deep longings help know God's desires for us, and how much God desires to be with us. And God, I believe, encourages us to "notice" and "name" these desires, in the same way that Jesus encouraged Bartimaeus, the blind beggar in the Gospels, to articulate his desire. "What do you want me to do for you?" he asked the blind man sitting by the roadside. "Lord, I want to see," says Bartimaeus.

Why does Jesus ask Bartimaeus a seemingly idiotic question? After all, Jesus knew that the man was blind! For one thing, Jesus may have wanted to offer him the freedom to ask, to give the man the dignity of choice, rather than simply healing him straight-away. For another, Jesus knew that recognizing our desires means recognizing God's desires for us. Jesus may have asked Bartimaeus what he wanted because our longings help us learn something about who we are. It's so freeing to say, "*This* is what I desire in life." Naming our desires may also make us more grateful when we receive the fulfillment of our hopes.

Expressing our desires brings us into a closer rela-tionship with God. Not naming them sets up a bar-rier. It would be like never telling your best friend your innermost thoughts. Your friend would remain distant. When we tell God our desires, our relation-ship with God deepens.

Desire is also a primary way people are led to dis-cover who they are and what they are meant to do. On the most obvious level, two people feel sexual, emotional and spiritual desire for one another, and in this way discover their vocations to love. A person feels an attraction to becoming a doctor, or a lawyer, or a teacher, and so discovers his or her vocation. Desire helps us find our way. But we first have to know them.

The deepest-held longings of our hearts are our holy desires. Not only desires for physical healing, as

Bartimaeus asked for (and as many ask for today) but also the hope for change, for growth, for a fuller life. And our deepest desires, those that lead us to become who we are, are God's desires *for us*. They are ways that God speaks to you directly, one way that, as St. Ignatius Loyola says, the "Creator deals directly with the creature." They are also one way that God fulfills God's own dreams for the world, by calling people to certain tasks.

Desire plays an enormous role in the life of a Jesuit. As novices, we were taught that our deep longings are important to notice. A young Jesuit who dreams of working with the poor and marginalized, for example, or studying Scripture, or working as a retreat director, will be encouraged to pay attention to his desires. Likewise, Jesuit superiors reverence these desires when making decisions about where to assign a particular Jesuit.

Sometimes in life, you might find yourself lacking the desire for something that you *want to desire*. Let's say you are living in a comfortable world with scant contact with the poor. You may say, "I know I'm *supposed* to want to live simply and work with the poor, but I have no desire to do this." Perhaps you know that you *should* want to be more generous, more loving, more forgiving, but don't desire it. How can you pray for that with honesty?

In reply, Ignatius would ask, "Do you at least have the *desire for this desire?*" Even if you don't want it, do you want to want it? Do you wish that you were the kind of person that wanted this? Even this can be seen as an invitation from God. It is a way of glimpsing God's invitation even in the faintest traces of desire.

Desire is a key part of Christian spirituality because desire is a key way that God's voice is heard in our lives. And our deepest desire, planted within us, is our Advent desire for Christ, the Desire of the Nations.

❧

Christ in Cambodia

Maria Montello

In Christ we have also obtained, an inheritance,
having been destined according to the purpose of
him who accomplishes all things according to his
counsel and will. . . .

—EPHESIANS 1:11

Standing in front of the class, Navy's (Nah-vee) eyes appeared to dart around behind closed eyelids fluttering haphazardly. Her head was tilted down slightly and her body not quite square with her classmates who looked on. Her hands were clenched. The air was thick; the anticipation palpable. Navy had uttered just the first few sentences of her presentation on the takeover of Phnom Penh by the Khmer Rouge. Then, she stood there frozen in silence, unable to speak. You could almost hear everyone's hearts hit the floor.

I do not know Navy's story. Perhaps I will someday. But to me, her professor, Navy was a marvel. On the first day of class, when I realized that sitting in the back of the classroom was a blind student, I wondered, "How did she make it up the 144 steps to my classroom, let alone have the sort of educational success to make it to the university?"

The realities of being disabled in Cambodia are harsh. It is thought by some that such a child must have been a bad person in a former life and hence been reincarnated in this "lesser form." Or, perhaps, the family had been cursed by someone in the village—someone with a grudge, someone to whom they owed a debt. In any case, the disability itself is only a part of the challenge.

Today, I thought about Navy's mother. She is Cambodian. Surely she was born into a society like today's which would have her see her daughter as less, her family as cursed. How was it that she had the state of mind and moral strength to raise the daughter who was standing there in front of that class? Navy's mother herself seemed not to have "inherited" this social sin—the sort of sin that has us believe some people are of less value than others just by virtue of the groups to which they belong, oftentimes through characteristics which they can't even control; the sort of conditioning that has us not only believe these things but, often unknowingly, pass them along to our children.

Not so Navy's mom. Through some grace—perhaps the care of her own parents—she escaped this "stain" and was able to raise a blind daughter who had made it to the best Cambodian university.

There is something special, it seems, about Navy's mother.

The Immaculate Conception is the day when we celebrate that there is something quite special about Mary, the mother of Jesus. Mary, the Church teaches, does not bear the stain of original sin, the sin which we all carry, the sin which gives us the predisposition to be judgmental and exclusionary, often unknowingly. Mary is "full of grace"—and from the very beginning of her life.

When Christ her Son stretched His arms on the cross, the crowds—the disciples, the Jews, the Roman soldiers—all looked on at Jesus, "King of the Jews," as the ultimate failure. Not so Mary. She knew: Her Son had stretched His arms from heaven to earth; He had brought God's own back; He had showed the world how to love.

The scene of Navy alone, frozen in front of the class played again and again in my head as I pedaled home that day. I saw the image of her standing there, dressed in her pressed skirt and jacket, knowing full well that all eyes were on her, citing haltingly only the first sentences of a presentation she had likely spent hours preparing. My heart was heavy as I thought about the disappointment Navy must have felt, the disappointment we all felt.

But then I thought about the realities of Navy's upbringing. I thought about the state of the Cambodian education system, where teachers struggle to serve any student let alone those who need special services. I thought that it was likely little had ever been done for Navy and less had ever been asked of her. I doubted that she had ever stood in front of a room full of her peers, let alone spoken, and in English. I was wrong, I realized, about what had happened that day. It was not a day of disappointment. That woman who stood before all of us was in fact courageous beyond measure. That day was Navy's triumph. Her mother would have been proud.

Asking for a Sign

Alan Jones

Some years ago, during Advent, I overheard a mother saying to another in the supermarket line: "It's a shame. These people dragging religion into Christmas and spoiling it for the children!" And it's understandable! The themes of Advent are in sharp contrast to the bustle and spending of Christmas.

The problem is that Christmas has lost its shock value. One of the great purposes of Advent is to help us recover that shock. What do you think was the hardest thing to believe for the early Christians? The shocking truth that everybody *matters.* You matter! What is the most real thing about you? The most real thing about you is that you are loved! The good news is that there is one human family and each one of us matters. St. Irenaeus tells us: "There is one human race wherein the mysteries of god are fulfilled." But the misdiagnosis—particularly poignant at Christmas with all that shopping!—of who we are, diminishes us. We are not essentially consumers, but adored creatures designed for communion with God and with each other. And as for gifts this year, God's own first gift to us is our own fragile self.

And Advent teaches us that the way back home to ourselves is through the door of repentance: a change of heart and mind, a correct diagnosis of the human condition. Repentance reconnects us with what matters and the big issue for this generation is *connection*—the Internet, the Web. Look at the world of Facebook! We have come to use of "the word 'connect' as believers use the word 'Jesus,' as if it were sacred in and of itself. . . . Connection is the goal. The quality of that connection, the quality of the information that passes through it, the quality of the relationship that connection permits—none of this is important . . . a lot of social networking software explicitly encourages people to make weak, superficial connections with each other. . . ."

Jaron Lanier, in his book, *You Are Not a Gadget*, points out that people reduce themselves because of

information technologies. "Information systems need
to have information in order to run, but information
underrepresents reality. It can't give us the full picture.
There is no perfect computer analogue for what we
call a 'person.' When life is turned into a data-base
there is degradation and we barely notice. When a
human being becomes a set of data on a website he
or she is reduced. Everything shrinks." Advent is a
revolution—a refusal to be degraded, diminished, un-
der-represented; an insistence that everyone matters.
And as for true connection, *you have to be somebody
before you can share yourself.* Advent and Christmas
are good news because the Gospel understands that
each of us is somebody, there is a mystery here. What
makes something fully real is you can't fully describe
it. You can't capture it in words. The way forward is
our recovering the truth that each of us is a mystery —
you are a mystery to the world and to yourself. You are
somebody! You are a gift.

So, Advent is vital as a preparation for the surprise
of Christmas! The surprise shows up great misdiagnosis of who we are. This is why some people, deep-
down, find this season depressing. Remember W.
H. Auden's point in his great Advent poem "For the
Time Being": This is a time when we unsuccessfully

try to love all our relations! Think of the passive and joyless mood that defines our present culture. Our flatness of soul is rooted in two main problems: first, our understanding of ourselves as essentially consumers, with the result that we think that everything is in principle fixable by our popping a pill or embracing some new technology; second, the depression that results from this misdiagnosis. Think of the cheerless and raucous exchanges in our politics, the bread-and-circuses flavor of our entertainments. Advent affirms that a right diagnosis of who we are (creatures made for communion and connection) can offer an antidote to our soul-sickness. The shock that each of us matters. The most real thing about us is that we are loved.

The really hard thing is not questions about the Virgin Birth or even about the divinity of Christ. The hard thing is for us to accept our own significance—even our own divinity. God knows, I'm not asking you to think of yourselves as God! But the Christmas story is as much about you as about God. Christmas is a celebration of your identity as a precious human being—in whom God chooses to dwell. God makes a home in you, in us—all of us. You are a bearer of glory. You, like Mary, are the container of the uncontainable, the bearer of God in the world. That's who you are. Adorable! Christmas heals the damage done by the great misdiagnosis of who we are.

The time for the baby is getting closer! The stirrings of new life give hope to the world. The real surprise of Christmas is being able to experience yourself as gift—experiencing yourself as pregnant with new life. We love babies because a baby is a sign of possibility. We look at a new-born baby and think—even if only for a moment—that there is a chance that the human race might make it after all! The baby, who cannot speak a word, is the Word of God! It's absurd. Yet there is the deepest of truths here. It's true.

Rabbi Lionel Blue, just after WWII, was convenor of *Beth Din*, the Reformed Jewish ecclesiastical court here in the U.K. His job was to try to apply rules, some archaic, to actual situations. "As we listened to our clients' stories, we realized what a gap had grown up between our pre-war religion and post-war reality." The job was somewhat restricting and claustrophobic, so Rabbi Blue decided with a refugee friend Eva to found an unusual congregation. The mirror image of the ecclesiastical court. There were no forms to fill in and everyone was welcome.

"No questions were asked about anyone's religious status, or about their personal relationships, whether single, divorced, or bereaved—or with no marriages at all. . . . If they wanted a Jewish Sabbath evening with candles, cinnamon cakes, company and blessings, they were welcome, and if they did not, they could walk out whenever they wished. We also asked them to add something to the supper table if they could. . . . They were all kinds, even some well-set-up Jews, pillars-of-society Jews, Jews living with Protestants, Catholics, Buddhists, and Jews who kept very non-kosher company indeed—and of course their partners came too, and received an even bigger welcome, not to convert them but because they might feel strange. There were half-Jews, quarter-Jews, one-eighth Jews . . . to these we added a Christian evangelical choir, who were so decent that they didn't try to convert anyone there, except by being the decent Christians that they were."

An odd assortment of people including one man "who said he was the Holy Spirit and locked himself in the broom cupboard, and some who took one look at us and left in disgust. . . ."

He goes on, "I could have cried with relief. At last I had found a temporary religious home, and Judaism was doing what it does best, turning the religious ragtag and bobtail of a big city into a family, even a sort of holy family." What will you do in the next few days until Christmas Eve? Visit the Crèche—with the gifts of your heart's hunger? Allow Joy to be born in you. Allow yourself to be loved and adored. Come as you are. Accept the gracious work of God to turn us—all of us without exception—into a family; yes, even a sort of holy family.

No one is turned away from the synagogue of the unqualified! Everyone is welcome. If you feel unqualified you know that you're in the right place!

Advent in Peru

Larry Rich

He will also strengthen you to the end . . .
—I CORINTHIANS I:8

On the one hand, today's readings articulate the hope that God will enter human history directly to save us in our time of great trouble—even if it is to save us from ourselves. On the other hand, there is the caution that when such an event should occur, we had better be prepared for the moment of "apocalypse" — from the Greek for "the lifting of the veil" —the moment of truth. Hope and getting ready: two elements we have long associated with Advent.

Despite the fact that popular culture and our own

sometimes childlike religious mindset may tend to imagine divine intervention as something occurring at the end of time and perhaps in a very fantastic way, there are less spectacular instances of revelation in the here-and-now. These tend to happen in the midst of genuine crises; and we will understand them only if we are prepared to see them. However, as many missioners would attest after serving in places where it can feel like instability is the norm, our vision remains obscured by the veil unless we are open to truth appearing in unlikely places. In times of crisis, we have learned, it is people who are poor who help us to open our eyes.

In 1992 in Lima, Peru, I witnessed what I would say qualifies as such a moment. I worked at a church human rights center during the harsh years of an unconventional war between the Shining Path, a group given to terrorist tactics, and the de facto government dictatorship with death squads. We used to talk about being caught between "two devils." As Peru's Truth and Reconciliation Commission later confirmed, each side killed some 30,000 people. By 1992, there was a pervasive sense of desperation over whether the violence would ever end. We heard stories daily of brutality by both the military and the Shining Path.

It did not seem totally inconceivable that Lima would eventually end up falling like Phnom Penh—with the Shining Path taking on the role of the Khmer Rouge. After over a decade in which many good people had died, we spoke about having way too many more martyrs.

Despite death threats and assassinations, many community leaders in the poorest barrios, especially the women, carried on with efforts to improve the lives of their neighbors. One of these was Maria Elena Moyano, who led an association of comedores populares—communal kitchens where people could gather to get a nutritious meal and children could get milk. These comedores were sometimes the target of terrorist bombings, and Maria Elena criticized the hypocrisy of the Shining Path's alleged people's revolution. On February 15, 1992, Maria Elena herself was assassinated by the Shining Path, her body blown to pieces by dynamite.

What happened next was as clear a breakthrough of hope in the midst of darkness as I have ever seen. At Maria Elena's open-air funeral Mass in her poverty-stricken part of town, there was great tension—soldiers ringed the area. Everyone feared reprisal from the Shining Path for what was seen as an act of defiance. As a result, many of the few hundred people present were human rights and aid workers from outside the barrio.

It was said at the Mass that they tried to scatter her remains to the four winds with explosives, but instead they sowed seeds of life.

When the funeral procession began the two-mile or so march by foot to the local cemetery it passed homes and side streets, and people began to pour out and swell its ranks until the time it arrived at the burial spot it numbered some 30,000 people and stretched as far down the road as one could see. Courage was being shown to the rest of Peruvian society by the marchers, mostly people without means and vulnerable in plain sight to the "thousand eyes" with which the Shining Path claimed to menacingly watch.

A public outcry followed in Peru that had not been heard in all those years. The news media invited community leaders, especially the women from the barrio organizations, as guests and interviewees on many of its programs. It was a rare moment in which the secular media seemed to have become the voice of the voiceless. It was as if middle and upper class Peruvians had perhaps begun to learn wisdom from those never considered important. Maybe the strength that kept the country from dissolving into chaos was found in the previously ignored efforts in poor communities to sustain life.

Within the same year, the leader of the Shining Path was captured, and he remains in prison to this day. His cult-like revolutionary organization fell apart. The government minister responsible for the death squads joined him in the same jail some years later. The dictatorial president has been imprisoned since 2007 for human rights violations.

The barrio organizations continue to this day, resilient in the face of challenges in affirming the dignity of all. Women's voices are heard more clearly now as Peruvians chart their future—for those who have ears to hear.

As we pass through our own kind of unending Advent of widespread unemployment and unprecedented economic inequality, are we prepared to see hope and the Spirit's truth in people and places where we have never looked before?

𓅰

A Familiar, Sweet Hunger

Phyllis Tickle

Christmas! Who's to say when it really begins or really ends? It's a delicious and teasing promise in a child's after-Halloween November, just as it is a familiar, sweet hunger in almost every grandparent's entire autumn. For both of them, as for most of the rest of us in between, it is also, once it is over and done, a sustaining memory that carries us safely for a quarter of every year forward into the grace-filled days of Spring and Easter.

Of necessity, of course, the Church, over the centuries, has tried to neaten the whole thing up a bit, or at least to define it a bit more cogently. It is, as we all know, the business of formal religion to do such as that from time to time. Yet looked at objectively,

most of what the ecclesial centuries have really accomplished, on this one issue at least, is some kind
of joyful, but still official and sanctioned, recognition
that Christmas can't be confined or restricted or cur-
tailed. It just wants to go longer than one day or one
small cache of days, just as its story is determined to
exceed any and all of our usual demarcations of literary time and categories.

So the Church in her infinite wisdom centuries
ago conceded the field by the simple expedient of ex-
panding it. There are, for instance, the four weeks of
Advent created to assure us that The Day and The
Event are indeed coming and that they are to be en-
joyed not only with a very human anticipation, but
also with a preparatory and sacred regimen of watching and waiting—of prayers and candles and readings
from Holy Writ.

And that regimen indeed preoccupies and sustains
us just as surely as it prepares us for the happy morning, four Sundays and usually a few days later, when
Christmas Day does dawn, and the great liturgies
and stories of the Church are heard ringing through
the ages and from ten thousand thousand naves and
chancels across Christendom.

But not yet satisfied, we cry out in our interrupted

December for yet another few days of quiet and worship and candle-lit celebration . . . for almost another fortnight of remembering and honoring and considering those who, by their actions and their faith, were the first to attest to the truths of Christmas. We do this until, at last, we stand firmly planted in January and watch in a sense of consummating beauty as three kings of a foreign and distant Orient yet once again proclaim this Child as King of humanity and of the Ages.

Yet all of this is not the whole of what wants to be said about Christmas. It is especially not the whole of wants saying in such times as ours. Rather, there is that other part, the part that must be acknowledged, if we are to be fully grateful: namely, that holy seasons, like holy days, are not so much established by the Church as they are provided us by the rhythms and seasons of life itself and then lovingly dressed by the Church in her narratives and symbols, in her drama and aesthetics, her nostalgia and transport. That is, liturgy gives objective form and inviolate, sustaining sanction to what both the mind and heart already know.

And the result always is that, so dressed and so sanctioned, holy days—and especially the blessedly long, appointed ones of Christmastide—become a community; or perhaps better said, they become a borderless space where shared awe becomes community across the aching caverns of the intervening centuries and despite doctrinal divisions and varying theological persuasions. In that holy space of liturgically-mentored time, as in no other, our experiencing, both individual and corporate, becomes the bonding of our lives, one with another, even as it teaches us ever more and more how to speak to each other in the lingua franca of the Spirit.

All of which is to say that, with the passing of my years, I have grown more and more grateful for the Church herself, for her beauty and her constancy, for her faithfulness as curator of the Story, for the width of her consoling arms and the drama of her vision. Thus it is that my own quiet prayer for Christmas has shrunk over the years into the most simple of petitions:

I pray that as surely as the Church blesses us in this life, we may be ever more and more blessing her with our joy in this and all the coming Christmastides of our own temporal lives.

Amen.

Advent

Mary Jo Salter

Wind whistling, as it does
in winter, and I think
nothing of it until

it snaps a shutter off
her bedroom window, spins
it over the roof and down

to crash on the deck in back,
like something out of Oz.
We look up, stunned—then glad

to be safe and have a story,
characters in a fable
we only half-believe.

Look, in my surprise
I somehow split a wall,
the last one in the house

we're making of gingerbread.
We'll have to improvise:
prop the two halves forward

like an open double door
and with a tube of icing
cement them to the floor.

Five days until Christmas,
and the house cannot be closed.
When she peers into the cold

interior we've exposed,
she half-expects to find
three magi in the manger,

a mother and her child.
She half-expects to read
on tablets of gingerbread

a line or two of Scripture,
as she has every morning
inside a dated shutter

on her Advent calendar.
She takes it from the mantel
and coaxes one fingertip

under the perforation,
as if her future hinges
on not tearing off the flap

under which a thumbnail picture
by Raphael or Giorgione,
Hans Memling or David

of apses, niches, archways,
cradles a smaller scene
of a mother and her child,

of the lidded jewel-box
of Mary's downcast eyes.
Flee into Egypt, cries

the angel of the Lord
to Joseph in a dream,
for Herod will seek the young

child to destroy him. While
she works to tile the roof
with shingled peppermints,

Goodness and Light

I wash my sugared hands
and step out to the deck
to lug the shutter in,

a page torn from a book
still blank for the two of us,
a mother and her child.

≈

Would It Be Okay
if You Hugged Me?
What a Tearful Teenage Boy
Taught Me about Advent

Sarah Thebarge

I flew to Houston over the weekend to speak at the Conspire Conference. I stood on a stage looking out over a few hundred students in grades 6 through 12, telling them my story of having breast cancer in my 20s.

I talked to them about what a dark season of life it was for me. The chemo and radiation were difficult, but on top of that I also lost a good friend to cancer, I was out of work for seven months, while in my apartment building's parking lot, my car was hit by a truck, and my boyfriend broke up with me. After all of that, I ended up in the hospital with a raging lung infection and a good chance that I would die.

On the nights I spent in the hospital, I'd lie awake and stare at the ceiling and wonder where God was. "Do you see me? Do you love me? Do you care about what's happening in my life?" I prayed. "And if you see me and love me and care about my life, why don't you come down and make this all go away?"

I told them how I eventually got better and moved from Connecticut to Oregon to start over. And every Sunday, I'd go to church and pray for God to find me because I felt so lost. For six months I prayed that same prayer, and then one Sunday I realized that the love of God is higher, longer, wider, and deeper than anything that happens in this world. And so not only was I now found by God, but never—even for a single second—had I ever been lost.

Around that time, I also met a Somali refugee woman and her girls on the train one afternoon. I ended up getting involved with their family, writing a blog about the adventure of helping them adjust to life in America, and turning the blog into a book called *The Invisible Girls* so I could use the proceeds to start a college fund for the five Somali girls.

I told the students how God worked everything for good—because I never would've been in Portland if my life on the East Coast hadn't fallen apart. And I never would've recognized the desperate look in the Somali woman's eyes except that it was exactly the same look I'd had in my eyes when I landed in Portland after losing everything but my life.

God had seemed absent, hiding in the shadows of painful circumstances. But it turns out he was with me all the time, and was taking each horrible, painful detail and working it for good.

At the close of the talk, I looked at the students and said, "I promise you that at some point in your life, something will happen that is difficult and painful. Something that you don't understand, that you don't want, that you don't like. And in that moment, you're going to think that God doesn't love you, that he's abandoned you, and forgotten all about you.

"And some of you are there right now—you've lost someone you loved, or a relationship ended badly, or you're getting bullied mercilessly. And maybe it seems so bad that the best way out is to end your life.

"But you are here tonight just to hear me tell you this: God. Loves. You.

"He sees you, he cares about you, and even when

you don't feel him near you, He's holding onto you every step of the way. And he's going to work this all out for good."

After I prayed for the students, I left the stage and the worship band began to play. One of the organizers met me backstage and led me to a table in the lobby where I was going to do a book signing.

When the kids were dismissed from the session, they got in line to buy a copy of *The Invisible Girls* and get it signed. A small girl, who was barely four feet tall, waited in line until it was her turn to come up to the table. "I don't have the money to buy your book," she said quietly. "But could you sign my name tag?"

One of the youth leaders ran and grabbed a permanent marker, and I signed her laminated name tag. Several other kids saw what was going on, and came over to get their name tags signed, too. Others came over and asked to take a picture with me.

After twenty minutes, everyone had come through the line, and the lobby emptied as the kids went to their next session.

And then an overweight teenage boy with thick glasses came up to the table clutching a copy of my book to his chest. He handed it to me to sign, which I did, and then I gave it back to him. Instead of walking away, he stood there in front of me without saying anything, and tears welled up in his eyes.

Finally, he broke the silence. "Would it be okay if you hugged me?" he asked.

I walked around the table and held my arms out. He wrapped his arms around my waist and clung to me.

"God sees you, God loves you, God cares about you," I whispered. And I could feel his shoulders shaking as he cried.

During Advent, I've been thinking a lot about Immanuel, God with us. And I've been thinking a lot about how, as his followers, we get to live out the incarnation for each other. We get to be the tangible presence of Jesus in this world—a presence that shines light and makes peace and whispers love.

We get to be his feet that walk the extra mile, his eyes that look on even the most messy, marginalized people with love; and his arms that wrap around self-conscious, bullied, lonely teenage boys.

We get to whisper into the aching ears of this world, "God sees you. God loves you. God cares about you. Yes—even you."

One or Two Things about Christmas

Annie Dillard

Let me mention
one or two things about Christmas.
Of course, you've all heard
that the animals talk
at midnight:
a particular elk, for instance,
kneeling at night to drink,
leaning tall to pull leaves
with his soft lips,
says, alleluia.

That the soil and freshwater lakes
also rejoice,
as do products
such as sweaters
(nor are plastics excluded
from grace),
is less well known.
Further:
the reason
for some silly-looking fishes,
for the bizarre mating
of certain adult insects
or the sprouting, say,
in a snow tire
of a Rocky Mountain grass,
is that the universal
loves the particular,
that freedom loves to live
and live fleshed full,
intricate, and in detail.

God empties himself
into the earth like a cloud.
God takes the substance, contours
of a man, and keeps them,

dying, rising, walking
and still walking
wherever there is motion.

At night in the ocean
the sponges are secretly building.
Once, on the Musselshell,
I regenerated an arm!
Shake hands. When I stand
the blood runs up.

On what bright wind
did God walk down?
Swaying under the snow,
reeling minutely,
revels the star-moss,
pleased.

Expectation of
Our Blessed Mother

Mother Mary Joseph Rogers, MM

"O Dawn of the East, brightness of the light eternal and Sun of Justice, come and enlighten them that sit in darkness and in the shadow of death."

Mary awaits with eager expectancy the birth of her Child, as mothers are wont to do, and we look upon her with marveling wonder and delight because of the working of God's mysteries through her and with tender compassion for all she is called upon to endure.

Her whole life had been a preparation for this unfolding miracle of grace. We think of her own birth as of an exquisite flower budding from seemingly barren stock, destined to spread its fragrance over the whole earth, and then as incense to rise up to heaven. Mary really knew very little of the life an ordinary child should have in a family, surrounded by affection and warmed by endearments. Her years in the temple, all formative ones, were spent in the service of God; her divinely directed soul, her lovely humility preparing itself—if only God would permit her such a privilege—to be the handmaid who would bear the long-expected Messiah. Then came Gabriel with his strange, stupendous, awful annunciation, "Hail Mary, full of grace, the Lord is with thee," and heaven and earth hung breathless on the words of this young maid on whose fiat depended humanity's redemption through the Incarnation. Mary gave the word, selflessly, lovingly, fearfully: "Be it done unto me according to Thy word." She would be God's handmaid, not because she had ever dreamed of this for herself, but because she knew God willed it should be so.

No one of us, I am sure, can appreciate the cataclysmic effect of that moment on Mary's soul. Did she realize, from a natural point of view, what her fiat involved, the suffering she would undergo, the misunderstanding? I presume she did not, and that the revelation of the consequences of her act formed no small part of the glorious heroism of her acceptance of them. We may be sure, too, that the Divine indwelling Child strengthened her soul and tempered the sweetened trials as they came, so that her joy no man could take from her.

Mary's visit to her cousin, Elizabeth, is but one instance of the sweet charity and selflessness that must have marked her days. Fatigue, distance, inconvenience, difficult travel: none of these could hold her back when another needed what she had to give. The richest fruit of that visit of Mary to her aged cousin Elizabeth—most likely the important part of God's designs in inspiring this—was the sanctification of John the Baptist in his mother's womb. In response to Elizabeth's inspired cry, "Blessed art thou among women and blessed is the fruit of thy womb," we hear the joyous Magnificat of Our Lady: "My soul doth magnify the Lord . . ."

So the months passed, and now we behold our Lady, her days almost accomplished, in joyful expectation of the appearance of the Sun of Justice, her own flesh and blood made divine through God's omnipotence. What were her thoughts? Were they wondering ones, as to what manner of child her little Son would be? What would be the color of His eyes and hair and would He really be the fairest of the children of men? And, thoroughly versed as she was with the prophecies, did she vision with sword-pierced heart the Lamb that was to be slain, the Lamb without blemish, her own adorable beloved Child, whom she was about to show forth to the world that would so ill-treat Him?

Doubtless both thoughts came to her, and she would gladly have kept her treasure hidden beneath her heart in safe shelter—yet, because she had freely made herself the handmaid of the Lord, her soul remained tranquil and at peace, eager and ready to co-operate in the Holy Trinity's plan for the redemption of humanity.

Mary's mood of expectancy is communicated to us. We know that Christ will come forth from her to be with us, for His delight is to be with the children of men. We shall look upon Christ as she did. Mary is about to make a supreme sacrifice, to begin that separation of herself from her Son which will culminate on Calvary, while we are preparing to receive into our hearts Him who is come to serve us with no thought of cost and to welcome us as victims of love. Mary's seeming loss is our sure gain.

We can only dimly realize how glorious and how sweetly beautiful a temple of God Mary has been as she cradled Christ within her. What can we say to describe the temple into which each of us will welcome him on Christmas Day? We have seen many Advents come and go, laden for the most part, with broken resolutions and unfulfilled promises. Year after year we have longed for Christmas and the Christ Child's presence in the crib. More especially, we have yearned daily for His advent into our own hearts. But yearnings and longings are futile unless they spur us on to action.

If we truly desire a royal visit, we prepare a fitting reception for the expected guest. So should it be with our desire to have Christ the King, the center of all hearts, come and dwell with us. What preparation do we make for such a royal friend? Is our heart like Mary's—a lovely tabernacle fashioned from our earliest childhood and richly embellished over the years? What have we done to beautify it in the past? More pertinent still, what have we done this past year? What has been our life of service, our life of prayer and sacrifice? Can we rejoice in them as we eagerly expect Jesus to come, to be reborn, as it were in our souls? Are our hearts truly hungry for Him? If so, how shall we appease that hunger?

December 22, 1949

~

True Happiness

Alfred Delp, SJ

What actually is happiness, true happiness? Philosophers have defined it as contentment with one's lot. That definition may fit certain aspects of the happy state but it certainly does not describe true happiness. If it did how could I possibly be happy in my present circumstances?

As a matter of fact we may ask ourselves whether it is worthwhile wasting time on an analysis of happiness. Is happiness not one of the luxuries of life for which no room can be found in the narrow strip of privacy which is all we have left when war occupies almost the whole of our attention? Certainly it would seem to be so in a prison cell, a space covered by three paces in each direction, one's hands fettered, one's heart filled with longings, one's head full of problems and worries.

Yet it does happen, even under these circumstances, that every now and then my whole being is flooded with pulsating life and my heart can scarcely contain the delirious joy there is in it. Suddenly, without any cause that I can perceive, without knowing why or by what right, my spirits soar again and there is not a doubt in my mind that all the promises hold good. This may sometimes be merely a reaction my defense mechanism sets up to counter depression. But not always. Sometimes it is due to a premonition of good tidings. It happened now and then in our community during a period of hardship and nearly always it was followed by an unexpected gift due to the resourcefulness of some kind soul at a time when such gifts were not customary.

But this happiness I am speaking of is something quite different. There are times when one is curiously uplifted by a sense of inner exaltation and comfort. Outwardly nothing is changed. The hopelessness of the situation remains only too obvious; yet one can face it undismayed. One is content to leave everything in God's hands. And that is the whole point. Happiness in this life is inextricably mixed with God. Fellow creatures can be the means of giving us much pleasure and of creating conditions which are comfortable and delightful, but the success of this depends upon the extent to which the recipient is capable of recognizing the good and accepting it. And even this capacity is dependent on our relationship with God.

Only in God are we capable of living fully. Without God we are permanently sick. Our sickness affects both our happiness and our capacity for happiness. That is why, when they still had time for leisure people made so much noise about their happiness. And in the end even that was forbidden. Their world became a prison which claimed them so completely that even happiness was made an excuse for further encroachment on their liberty.

In order to be capable of leading a full life a person must stand in a certain relationship to God and obey certain rules. And the capacity for true happiness and joyful living is also dependent on certain conditions of human life, on a serious attitude toward God. Where life does not unfold in communion with God it becomes grey and sordid, calculating and joyless.

How must we live in order to be, or to become, capable of happiness? The question is one which ought to occupy us nowadays more than ever before. Humans should take their happiness as seriously as they take themselves. And they ought to believe God and their own hearts when, even in distress and trouble, they have an intuitive feeling that they were created for happiness. But this entails certain clear convictions. For a full and satisfying life we must know what it is all about. We must have no doubts about being on the right road with all the saints to back us up, and divine strength to support us. Such a life is a dedicated one, conscious of being blessed and touched by God himself.

How must we live in order that happiness may overflow our hearts and shine from our eyes, making our countenance radiant? How must we live to ensure that the work of our hands, conscientiously competent, will be crowned with success?

The liturgy for today gives us five conditions for the achievement of happiness and the capacity to enjoy it. In weighing up these conditions we have to examine our conscience and at the same time meditate on some of the historical causes for joylessness in modern life. We have to ask ourselves how it comes about that humanity has been fobbed off with a substitute so blatant that, were they not soul-sick, rightthinking people would never have been taken in by it.

Perhaps too this will give us an inkling of how matters stood with great people of the past who were really capable of happiness—whose eyes were so clear that they detected happiness everywhere. The sun song of St. Francis is not a lyrical dream but a creative expression of that inner freedom which made it possible for him to extract the last ounce of pleasure from every experience and to perceive it in the successful issue of everything he undertook.

The conditions of happiness have nothing whatever to do with outward existence. They are exclusively dependent on our inner attitude and steadfastness, which enable us, even in the most trying circumstances, to form at least a notion of what life is about.

☙

Be Vigilant at All Times

David Davis

One of my earliest memories of school days when I was a child comes from a morning in first or second grade when we had to prepare a Peterson's Writing Specimen: a half-sheet of white paper, wide-lined, the class writing a series of letters and words in cursive, using ball point pens. Our very best effort in penmanship then sent away to the Peterson people who would send back the best in the class for proper accolades. I worked very carefully and did the best I could, the best ever, and I came to the end and had to sign my name. Bottom right, last line, I signed "David . . . David" I had to start all over. I was crushed. The second paper wasn't as good. I had to rush. Truth is, that one half-sheet of paper was the best penmanship of my life. My handwriting has never been any better, in fact, it has continually over forty some years only become worse. My elementary school handwriting do-over.

Look around the sanctuary this morning. It looks, it sounds, it feels like Advent. Wreath. Purple. Banners. Hymns. Familiar biblical texts. Tree lighting in Palmer Square. Horse-drawn carriage rides around town. Crowds for shopping. The Salvation Army bell ringer. Counting days until Christmas. Here we go again! Advent. The beginning of the new year when it comes to the church calendar: Advent. Christmas. Epiphany. Lent. Holy Week. Good Friday. Easter. Eastertide. Pentecost. Birth of Jesus. Life of Jesus. Death of Jesus. Resurrection. Holy Spirit . . . and back again. Here we go, again. Come, o come Emmanuel! Come thou long-expected Jesus! Even so, come Lord Jesus! Advent. One big do-over! A re-write for those in English class. A mulligan for the golfers. In Harry Potter, yet another book. In music, a reprise . . . the return to the first notes of the melody. It's Advent. Here we go . . . again.

But it doesn't get any better. I'm not talking about our singing, or the opportunities here at the church, or the artwork, or how we do our worship, or one year's theological theme compared to another, or how well we teach and include our children, or how we do in welcoming newcomers this time of year, or when it comes to lifting up mission and outreach opportunities and God's call to us to be the body of Christ in the world. None of that is what I mean when I say it doesn't get any better. You know what I mean: life, the world, the struggles, the suffering, the kingdom coming on earth as it is in heaven kind of thing . . . the big picture out there, maybe in here (in the heart) . . . it doesn't get any better. Advent and this do-over thing!!

Most every year when we get to Advent, the gospel reading tells of the teaching of Jesus regarding the Coming of the Son of Man. As in this morning's reading from Luke. *"They will see the Son of Man coming in a cloud with power and great glory . . . be alert at all times, praying that you may have the strength to escape all these things that will take place, and to stand before the Son of Man."* Jesus and his Second Coming. You recognize that Advent theme. We've been here so many times before; celebrating again the birth of Jesus while looking in faith to his coming again! In betwixt and between, the already and the not yet. Must be Advent.

The Coming of the Son of Man. The Second Coming of Jesus. The reference to Christ's coming again on Advent I, it always comes with this apocalyptic flair. You heard it in the reading: *"Signs in the sun, the moon, and the stars . . . distress among the nations, the roaring of the sea, fear and foreboding, the powers of the heavens will be shaken . . . don't let that day catch you unexpectedly like a trap. For it will come upon all who live on the face of the whole earth."* And preachers and teachers go to great lengths to try to explain biblical, apocalyptic literature, and the parallels to the Book of Daniel and the Book of Revelation, and the history rooted in the destruction of the Temple and the fall of Jerusalem and the already and the not yet of biblical prophecy in the context of the unique genre of apocalyptic, complete with warnings against those who want to predict and sell books and go political and decide who gets to go and who is left behind. Preachers and teachers like me go to great lengths to try to explain apocalyptic literature in the Bible every year, every Advent, every time we go through this again. Every do-over.

When you stop and think about it, such apocalyptic consciousness is not just about biblical literature. Nor is it only in video games and fantasy novels. More than 6,000 American soldiers have been killed in Iraq and Afghanistan. More than 30,000

American men and women have been wounded. Civilian casualties in Iraq alone as a result of war and ongoing internal violence by some estimates exceeded 200,000. South Africa is a nation of 45 million people. In 2007 5.7 million were infected with HIV/AIDS. According to US Census statistics, 39.8 million people in 2008 lived in poverty. 14.1 million of those were children. 1 in 5 children in the United States live in poverty. Statistics of apocalyptic proportions. Words with apocalyptic connotations are everywhere. Words like rampage, surge, violence: workplace, family, random violence, war on drugs, pandemic. And the genre and language of apocalyptic has made a rousing debut in the healthcare debate coming from every side of the aisle. Preachers don't prime your apocalyptic imagination. The world already takes care of that.

It's never that far from home, either, far from life in here, I mean. Every time we gather as the Body of Christ, you know there is someone whose daily battle is beyond description, someone who is living a story of endurance and perseverance, a family who is pinning the needle in struggle, someone now labeled a "surviving spouse." Every time we come here there are words from your life and mine that start to sound like this biblical literature, they start to sound apocalyptic: reduction in force, downsized, metastatic, Alzheimer's, credit crisis, hospice, long term care, chronic pain, rock bottom, despair. I guess what I am trying to say is that the longer I serve in pastoral ministry the less I think I have to explain the literature of apocalyptic. You already know; not because of movies or video games or the evening news or politics but because of life. Life out there and life in here. Life and how when Advent comes around, yeah, it doesn't seem to be getting any better.

When these things take place, Jesus said, when that's how it feels, when the Advent do-over just isn't working . . . right then, stand up and raise your head, because your redemption is drawing near. Your redemption. Your salvation. Your liberation. Your forgiveness. Your new life. Your resurrection hope. Your life forever in the kingdom of God. It is drawing near. God draws near. Jesus draws near. Not just because the calendar marches on, not just because we're on the clock, but because life happens. Not because we've come around to Advent again, but because once again we come to Advent with a certain fullness to life that demands and cries out for the very fullness of God.

Stand up. Raise your head. Your redemption is drawing near. God draws near. Jesus draws near. Not just then, now. Stand up. Raise your head, not just to see the horizon, but to experience his presence now. The difference between apocalyptic fantasy in film, and a fascination with post-apocalyptic survival, the difference between all of that and the apocalyptic promise of God, is the tense, the timing, the real presence of Christ Jesus when life is happening now.

Real presence. Christ is present here, just as he promised. Christ promises, "I am here. This is my body broken for you. This is my blood shed for you. Forgiveness. Liberation. Salvation. Redemption. Take. Eat. Drink. Stand up. Raise your head. Jesus nears. The sacramental, apocalyptic promise of God.

If you were to gather all this literature of scripture together, all the apocalyptic writings of scripture, one collector's set, special edition, it would of course end with the Book of Revelation. And right at the end, before the benediction that concludes the Book of Revelation, right before "The grace of the Lord Jesus be with all the saints. Amen." Right there at the end, Revelation 22:20: *"Come, Lord Jesus!"* *"Even so, come Lord Jesus"* in the King James.

Come, Lord Jesus. It's not a victory shout. It's not

a political slogan that paves the way for four more years. It's not a billboard or a movie trailor intended for an endtime scenario. It's a gut-wrenching, heart-felt plea. A prayer. Dare we say it, a demand! Come, Lord Jesus. A prayer for the Advent do-over, especially when it's not getting any better. Not getting any better—you know what I mean. Come Lord Jesus. It is not "come and finish this all up!" It is "come, now, quickly, come right now!"

⁓

The Materialism of Santa Claus and the Spirituality of Baby Jesus

Leonardo Boff

One good day, the Son of God wanted to know how the boys and girls were, who in another time, when he was among us, "He touched and blessed," and of whom He had said: "let the children come to me because theirs is the Kingdom of God" (Luke 18:15-16).

Like in the old myths, He mounted a celestial ray and reached Earth a few weeks before the Nativity. He assumed the form of a street sweeper.

That way He could better see the people passing by, the well-illuminated stores, filled with things wrapped as gifts, and especially His smallest sisters and brothers who were walking around, not well dressed and many of whom were hungry, and begging. He became very sad because He understood that almost no one followed the words He had said: "who receives one of these children in my name, receives me" (Mark 9:37).

He also saw that no one spoke of the Baby Jesus who would come, secretly, on the night of the Nativity to bring gifts for the children. His place had been taken by a good natured old man, dressed in red, with a long beard and carrying a sack, who would constantly call out the silly refrain: "Ho, Ho, Ho, Santa Claus is here." Yes, he was in the streets and in the great stores, embracing the children and taking from his sack the gifts that the parents had bought and put there. It is said that he had come from far away, from Finland, mounted on a sleigh pulled by reindeer. The people had forgotten another little old man, this one a really good one: Saint Nicholas. From a wealthy family, on Nativity he would hand out gifts to poor children, saying that it was the Baby Jesus who sent it to them. No one would speak about all that. They only talked about Santa Claus, invented a little over one hundred years ago.

As sad as seeing the abandoned children in the streets, was seeing how people became giddy, seduced by the lights and the splendor of the gifts, and the thousands of things parents usually buy to give away on the occasion of the Nativity Eve meal.

The advertisements, mostly misleading, are shouted out loudly, arousing the desire of the children who run to their parents, asking them to buy them the things they have seen. The Jesus Child, dressed as a street sweeper, came to realize that everything the angels sang that night throughout the fields of Bethlehem, "we proclaim the joy that will also be for all the people, because today has been born a Savior. . . . Glory to God in the highest and peace on Earth to people of good will" (Luke 2:10-14) means nothing anymore. Love has been replaced by objects, and the joyfulness of God, who made Himself a child, had disappeared in the name of the pleasure of consumption.

Sad, He mounted another celestial ray, but before returning to heaven, He left a letter He had written for the children. They found the letter under the doors of their houses and, especially, of the huts in the outskirts of the city, called, favelas. The letter said:

Dear little brothers and sisters:

If on seeing the manger, you see there the Baby Jesus, with Joseph and Mary, and you are filled with faith in God who made Himself a child, a child like any of you, and who is God-brother who is always with you.

If you manage to see in the other boys and girls, especially in the poorest, the hidden presence of the Baby Jesus being born in them.

If you are capable of making the child hidden in your parents and the other grown ups you know be reborn, so that from them spring forth love, tenderness, caring and friendship instead of many gifts.

If on seeing the manger and seeing Jesus poorly dressed, almost naked, you remember so many other children who are equally poorly dressed, and you hurt deep in your heart because of this inhumane situation, and you want to share what you have with others and from now you wish to change these things when you are an adult, so that never again would there be boys and girls who cry of hunger and cold.

If when you discover the Magi who bring

gifts to the Baby Jesus you think that even the kings, the heads of state and other important persons of humanity come from all over the world to contemplate the greatness hidden in this small Child who cries in the hay.

If on seeing in the nativity scene the oxen and the donkey, the sheep, goats, dogs, the camels and the elephant, you think that the whole universe is also illuminated by the divine Child and that everything, the stars, suns, galaxies, stones, trees, fish, animals and all of us, the human beings, form the Great House of God.

If you see the sky and see the star with its luminous tail and remember that always there is a Star such as the one of Bethlehem over you, that accompanies, illuminates and shows you the better paths.

If you listen carefully and hear through your inner senses a soft and celestial music like that of the angels over the fields of Bethlehem, who announced peace on Earth.

Then, know that I, the Baby Jesus, am being born again and am renewing the Nativity. I will be always near, walking with you, crying with you and playing with you, until the day when all, humanity and universe, arrive to the House of God, who is Father and Mother of infinite goodness, to be eternally happy together as a great reunited family.

Signed: *The Baby Jesus*

Bethlehem, December 25, Year 1

꽃

The Jesus I Love

Mohandas Gandhi

*At the request of Christian fellow-passengers, Gandhi
gave the following talk on Christmas Day, 1931, while
sailing back to India after attending the Second Round
Table Conference in London.*

I shall tell you how, to an outsider like me, the
story of Christ, as told in the New Testament, has
struck. My acquaintance with the Bible began nearly
forty-five years ago, and that was through the New
Testament. I could not then take much interest in the
Old Testament, which I had certainly read, if only to
fulfill a promise I had made to a friend whom I happened to meet in a hotel. But when I came to the New
Testament and the Sermon on the Mount, I began to

understand the Christian teaching, and the teaching of the Sermon on the Mount echoed something I had learnt in childhood and something which seemed to be part of my being and which I felt was being acted up to in the daily life around me.

I say it seemed to be acted up to, meaning thereby that it was not necessary for my purpose that all were actually living the life. This teaching was nonretaliation, or nonresistance to evil. Of all the things I read, what remained with me forever was that Jesus came almost to give a new law—though he of course had said he had not come to give a new law, but tack something on to the old Mosaic law. Well, he changed it so that it became a new law—not an eye for an eye, and a tooth for a tooth, but to be ready to receive two blows when only one was given, and to go two miles when they were asked to go one.

I said to myself, this is what one learns in one's childhood. Surely this is not Christianity. For all I had then been given to understand was that to be a Christian was to have a brandy bottle in one hand and beef in the other. The Sermon on the Mount, however, falsified the impression. As my contact with real Christians, i.e., men living in fear of God, increased, I saw that the Sermon on the Mount was the whole of Christianity for him who wanted to live a Christian life. It is that Sermon which has endeared Jesus to me.

I may say that I have never been interested in a historical Jesus. I should not care if it was proved by someone that the man called Jesus never lived, and that what was narrated in the Gospels was a figment of the writer's imagination. For the Sermon on the Mount would still be true for me.

Reading, therefore, the whole story in that light, it seems to me that Christianity has yet to be lived, unless one says that where there is boundless love and no idea of retaliation whatsoever, it is Christianity that lives. But then it surmounts all boundaries and book teaching. Then it is something indefinable, not capable of being preached to men, not capable of being transmitted from mouth to mouth, but from heart to heart. But Christianity is not commonly understood in that way.

Somehow, in God's providence, the Bible has been preserved from destruction by the Christians, so-called. The British and Foreign Bible Society has had it translated into many languages. All that may serve a real purpose in the time to come. Two thousand years in the life of a living faith may be nothing. For though we sang, "All glory to God on High and on the earth be peace," there seems to be today neither glory to God nor peace on earth.

As long as it remains a hunger still unsatisfied, as long as Christ is not yet born, we have to look forward to Him. When real peace is established, we will not need demonstrations, but it will be echoed in our life, not only in individual life, but in corporate life. Then we shall say Christ is born. That to me is the real meaning of the verse we have sung. Then we will not think of a particular day in the year as that of the birth of the Christ, but as an ever-recurring event which can be enacted in every life.

And the more I think of fundamental religion, and the more I think of miraculous conceptions of so many teachers who have come down from age to age and clime to clime, the more I see that there is behind them the eternal truth that I have narrated. That needs no label or declaration. It consists in the living of life, never ceasing, ever progressing towards peace.

When, therefore, one wishes "A Happy Christmas" without the meaning behind it, it becomes nothing more than an empty formula. And unless one wishes for peace for all life, one cannot wish for peace for oneself. It is a self-evident axiom, like the axioms of

Euclid, that one cannot have peace unless there is in one an intense longing for peace all around. You may certainly experience peace in the midst of strife, but that happens only when to remove strife you destroy your whole life, you crucify yourself.

And so, as the miraculous birth is an eternal event, so is the Cross an eternal event in this stormy life. Therefore, we dare not think of birth without death on the cross. Living Christ means a living Cross, without it life is a living death.

[At the request of an American reporter, Gandhi added the following message of Christmas greetings.]

I have never been able to reconcile myself to the gaieties of the Christmas season. They have appeared to me to be so inconsistent with the life and teaching of Jesus.

How I wish America could lead the way by devoting the season to a real moral stocktaking and emphasizing consecration to the service of mankind for which Jesus lived and died on the Cross.

Christmas in Prison

Pedro Arrupe, SJ

It was Christmas night. My mind went back to so many happy Christmases, to the three masses which I was able to celebrate that night. What remembrances filled my mind! But none of all this was now possible. I was alone, without mass. Instead of Christmas it seemed more like Good Friday! Just then when my Christmas was being changed into the passion and that blessed night into a sad Gethsemane, I heard a strange sound near one of the windows. It was the soft murmur of many voices which, with muted accents, sought to escape detection. I began to listen. If any of you have been in prison waiting for a sentence, you would appreciate the anxiety with which I followed those sounds which were now of themselves becoming an immediate source of suspicion. Such are the fears that one feels within the four walls where one is detained.

Suddenly, above the murmur that was reaching me, there arose a soft, sweet, consoling Christmas carol, one of the songs which I had myself taught to my Christians. I was unable to contain myself. I burst into tears. They were my Christians who, heedless of the danger of being themselves imprisoned, had come to console me, to console their *Shimpu Sarna* (their priest), who was away that Christmas night which hitherto we had always celebrated with such great joy. What a contrast between that thoughtfulness and the injustice of senseless imprisonment!

The song with those accents and inflections which are not taught or learned poured forth from a touching kindness and sincere affection. It lasted for a few minutes; then there was silence again. They had gone and I was left to myself. But our spirits remained united at the altar on which soon after would descend Jesus. I felt that he also descended into my heart, and that night I made the best spiritual communion of all my life.

≈

The Surprise Child

James T. Keane

For many Christians it has perhaps become commonplace to view Advent as a season of inevitability, a ritual expectation of the birth of the Son of God, surely, but one that lacks suspense. We already know how the story will turn out, don't we? The Holy Family will make it to Bethlehem; they will find a manger; Jesus will be born; everything will run as planned and on schedule. Yet it is worthwhile to recall that Advent celebrates birth, one of the most vulnerable of human moments, and to remind ourselves that Jesus was an unexpected child: Mary had a different life planned for herself and Joseph, not to mention Joseph's own hopes and dreams for his family.

What must those cold final months of pregnancy

have been like for Mary, away from home and desperate for shelter? In our still male-centered world, we may think more of the coming of Jesus than of the worries and concerns of his mother, who knew a life we often do not admit, one surely full of confusion about her role as well as dreams and fears for her family's well-being and future. Do we give enough attention in our prayer and celebration to her interior life—this young woman called by forces she did not fully understand to give birth to a child whose coming was shrouded in so much mystery?

I am of an age where my friends and siblings seem to have acquired an incredible fecundity. Not a month goes by without the good news that one or more of them is expecting. Pregnancy involves uncertainty, of course, so they are careful not to make an announcement too soon. Often they communicate the news subtly. A friend declines a glass of wine at dinner, sisters start whispering in the corner at family gatherings, boxes of clothes reappear out of attics and closets, and suddenly everyone realizes the good news. Each time, though, there is worry, but more often than not it is the worry of middle-class Americans supported by family, society, and financial security. It is not the worry of an unmarried teenager living at subsistence level in a land under foreign military occupation; it is not that of a woman struggling to avoid public scandal, yet singing a hymn of hope in an environment more suggestive of its opposite.

The great German theologian Dietrich Bonhoeffer once called Mary's *Magnificat* "the most passionate, the wildest, one might even say the most revolutionary Advent hymn ever sung," not a Christmas carol or a recitation of pious treacle but a "hard, strong, inexorable song about collapsing thrones and humbled lords of this world, about the power of God and the powerlessness of humankind." The woman who sang that song was not the serene and half-asleep royal figure depicted in Western art over the centuries, but a young woman fully alive in history, whose answer to God had consequences both long-range and immediate for herself, her family, and the world.

Some have argued that the church would benefit from further reflection on Mary's yes at the Annunciation, acknowledging that a component of every pregnancy, expected or not, should be a woman's active choice to say yes to the child she will bear. That equation, however, works just as well turned on its head, because we as a church would also profit from reflection on what the angel Gabriel says to Mary in Luke's account: The Lord is with you. Do not be afraid. Even the most unplanned of pregnancies, Gabriel tells Mary (and us), enjoys divine protection and care. The implied message is a profound one: Yes, this situation you are in seems impossible, and no one can guarantee you and your child a life without suffering. But you and your child are part of a divine plan, and for this reason, you are never alone. An unexpected child can be treated as a liability or a mistake, not a birth to be anticipated with hymns and celebration, but a problem to be solved. Mary's response, though, is exemplary: she embraced her new reality and her new child.

In this Advent season, let us remember and be grateful for the yes Mary gave to that sudden visitor who brought such shocking news. For Mary's decision brought life to the world. The child she bore and reared has changed our fates forever. Perhaps the joy and gratitude we bring to the new arrivals in our world give us a starting point for loving Mary's son.

~~~

The Miracle of Christmas Bread

Rose Marie Berger

"Food brings people together."

Thursday night is baking night at Panadería El Latino on 11th Street. Early Friday morning, the bakers pull their weekend supply of *pan dulce* from the ovens. Racks and racks of *conchas, cuernos,* and *galletas*—in eye-popping yellows and pinks—are set out to cool. The entire street is redolent with yeast, cinnamon, and sugar.

From the outside this bakery looks like any another boarded-up building. "The only indication this isn't a crack den," one local points out, "is the overwhelmingly delicious smell of baked goods." El Latino distributes to corner *bodegas* across the metro D.C. area.

But, if you brave the exterior, you can get three sweet rolls for a buck. Bread of heaven!

Extending our tables to feed the multitudes is a practice Jesus asks us to imitate (Matthew 14:16). When Jesus hosted that feast for "more than 5,000" with "only five loaves and two fish," it was called a miracle. But the mystery wasn't in magic math. Rather this is a tale of two parties. In Matthew 14:13-21, the dilemma was that there was too little food and too many people. But in the preceding verses, there was too much food and too little *humanity*.

Matthew 14:1-12 tells the story of Herod's birthday party. Here, only the upper one percent, the elite and powerful, are gathered in a setting overflowing with the rarest wines, mountains of meat, and the finest breads. But Herodias' daughter demands a different dish. The main course is served to her on a platter: It is the head of John the Baptist.

These are the two "feedings" that Matthew juxtaposes. In Jesus' time, the economic 99 percent are abused by a market system controlled by an unaccountable power. The disciples neither understand the enormity of the problem nor the blasphemy inherent in the system.

"Send the crowds away," they say, "so that they

may go into the villages and buy food for themselves" (14:15). The disciples still believe the "market system" will solve the problem.

According to New Testament scholar Warren Carter, at the time "the emperor, and through him various gods, [was] responsible for blessing the empire with adequate food." Ceres, the goddess of grain, showed her approval of the Roman emperor by providing good grain harvests. But, as Juvenal contemptuously reminds, the government is trading cheap white bread for actual political power and distracting the people with "circuses."

Jesus' retort to his followers is categorical: "*You* give them something to eat."

Jesus acts as host to a Great Picnic. The disciples are taught how to serve. Jesus makes them practice extending the table, sharing the bread (14:18-19), rather than doing it for them. Bread for all, Jesus proclaims! It is God's will that hungry people be fed—but with a bread that satisfies.

The Christmas season is a time for feasting and celebrating. An English custom holds that a loaf of bread baked on Christmas Eve will cure the sick and heal the broken-hearted. An Orthodox table tradition requires the communal sharing of bread and honey.

First, the host dips a small piece of Christmas *krendel* in honey and salt, then approaches each dinner guest, starting with the eldest. "Christ is born," she says. "Let us adore him," responds the guest.

"Food sustains and enriches our life and cultures," writes Ched Myers, "yet when there is too little or too much of it, desperation or greed follow. Food brings people together, but also divides them. Table fellowship (with whom, and how, and what we eat) mirrors the inclusions and exclusions of the wider society."

This Christmas, let's fill our tables with simple foods. Set up extra chairs. Welcome the unexpected guest. Invite the stranger. Remind one another that Christ is born! And, when our bread is blessed and broken, call to mind Jesus' mandate to all disciples: "You give them something to eat."

~~

Do Not Be Afraid

Greg Kandra

In the late nineteenth century, one of the most sought-after realist portrait painters was a Frenchman by the name of James Tissot. He made his reputation painting society women and the wealthy in and around Paris. But at one point in his life, while doing research for a painting, he stepped inside a church. While there, he had a profound religious experience. He left a changed man, and devoted the rest of his life to spiritual and religious themes—including hundreds of paintings depicting scenes from the Bible, most famously, the life of Christ. The Brooklyn Museum has many of these sketches and watercolors, and they had an exhibit last year. They are beautiful, and moving.

They are also deeply human—none more so than a

work that has direct bearing on this Sunday's gospel. It is a surprising portrait of St. Joseph.

Joseph is shown at his carpenter's table, with tools scattered around him. His shop is small, cramped, planks and pieces of wood everywhere, shavings piled up on the floor. The windows look out onto the bustling streets of Nazareth, where townspeople are going about their business. But in the middle of all that stands Joseph, bent over his table, his bearded chin in his hand, deep in thought.

The painting's title says it all: "The Anxiety of Joseph."

We rarely think of him that way. But Tissot, as he often does, penetrated to the heart of his subject.

Maybe Tissot was showing Joseph the morning before he has the dream we just heard in Matthew's gospel. Or maybe it is the morning after —and he is coming to terms with what the angel has said, and what he must do.

But what we see in Tissot's picture—and what is hinted at in this gospel today—is a man more like us than we realize.

We tend to think of Joseph the way we see him in the manger scene outside our church, or on the cards we send, or the pageants that are staged. He is strong, stoic, patient—"righteous," as Matthew describes him.

But Tissot understood that the man betrothed to Mary was a man of worries, and apprehension, and even fear. This morning, I'd like to suggest that Joseph is also a man who speaks to our own time.

He is a man for our age—an Age of Anxiety.

He must have known economic uncertainty—wondering how he would support and sustain his family, running his own small business. He had to pay taxes—to "render unto Caeser." Like many people today, shortly after his son was born, Joseph and his family became refugees, immigrants in a foreign land—the land that had held his people as slaves. Joseph also lived with the threat of terror—a ruthless king bent on murdering children.

On a more personal level, Joseph knew the anxiety of any man about to become a father. He must have asked himself: *Am I ready for this? Am I good enough, strong enough, wise enough?* And then, confronting the very real possibility of scandal, Joseph must have had more than a few sleepless nights. How, he must have wondered, could he protect and spare the woman he loved?

And—like Mary, the woman he loved—he also

must have thought at some point: *This is not what I had planned. Everything is suddenly different.*

How many of us have said that about our own lives? How many of us have had to face, like Joseph, a confusing world with uncertainty, and doubt, and anxiety and fear?

How many of us have felt like the man in that Tissot drawing, frozen in place, while the world moves on around us, and we stand there and worry and wonder: what do I do? How will I get through this?

But into all that, in Joseph's complicated life, comes a voice in a dream.

"Do not be afraid. God is with us."

And his world—and ours—is changed.

In the middle of "the anxiety of Joseph" comes blessed reassurance—and a reminder that God's will sees beyond our fears, beyond our limitations.

When our lives can seem a nightmare, we cannot forget to dream.

When every demon seems to be making our lives hell, we cannot forget to listen for angels.

When our world has been turned upside down, we cannot forget to trust that God will make it right.

Again and again, the words come to us from the gospels, in times of confusion and doubt and anxiety.

"Do not be afraid."

That is the message to Joseph, to Mary, to the shepherds, to the apostles—and to us.

And in these last days of Advent, that is the great message the gospels leave us with as we light the last candle and sing "O Come, O Come Emmanuel." The light is brighter. God's presence is closer.

If you have any doubts about that, just think of Joseph, the great silent partner of the Holy Family, the man who doesn't utter a word in the gospels—but whose ability to trust, and to dream, and to listen speaks volumes.

In the end, the words of the angel echo down to us as the great defining message of Advent hope—banishing all fear, easing all anxiety.

"Do not be afraid. God is with us."

Into the Dark with God

Hans Urs von Balthasar

And the angel said to them,

> Be not afraid; for behold, I bring you Good
> News of a great joy that will come to all the
> people: for to you is born this day in the city
> of David a Savior, who is Christ the Lord.
> And this will be a sign for you: you will find
> a babe wrapped in swaddling clothes and
> lying in a manger (LUKE 2:10-12)

On Christmas night the shepherds are addressed
by an angel who shines upon them with the blinding glory of God, and they are very much afraid. The
tremendous, unearthly radiance shows that the an-

gel is a messenger of heaven and clothes him with an incontrovertible authority. With this authority he commands them not to be afraid but to embrace the great joy he is announcing to them. And while the angel is speaking thus to these poor frightened people, he is joined by a vast number of others, who unite in a "Gloria" praising God in heaven's heights and announcing the peace of God's goodwill to men on earth. Then, we read, "the angels went away from them into heaven." In all probability the singing was very beautiful and the shepherds were glad to listen; doubtless they were sorry when the concert was over and the performers disappeared behind heaven's curtain. Probably, however, they were secretly a little relieved when the unwonted light of divine glory and the unwonted sound of heavenly music came to an end, and they found themselves once more in their familiar earthly darkness. They probably felt like shabby beggars who had suddenly been set in a king's audience chamber among courtiers dressed in magnificent robes and were glad to slip away unnoticed and take to their heels.

But the strange thing is that the intimidating glory of the heavenly realm, which has now vanished, has left behind a human glow of joy in their souls, a

light of joyous expectation, reinforcing the heaven-
ward-pointing angel's word and causing them to set
out for Bethlehem. Now they can turn their backs
on the whole epiphany of the heavenly glory—for it
was only a starting point, an initial spark, a stimulus
leading to what was really intended; all that remains
of it is the tiny seed of the word that has been im-
planted in their hearts and that now starts to grow
in the form of expectation, curiosity and hope: "Let
us go over to Bethlehem and see this thing that has
happened, which the Lord has made known to us."
They want to see the word that has taken place. Not
the angel's word with its heavenly radiance: that
has already become unimportant. They want to see
the content of the angel's word, that is, the Child,
wrapped in swaddling clothes and lying in a manger.
They want to see the word that has "happened," the
word that has taken place, the word that is not only
something uttered but something done, something
that cannot only be heard but also seen.

Thus the word that the shepherds want to see is
not the angel's word. This was only the proclamation
(the kerygma, as people say nowadays); it was only
a pointer. The angels, with their heavenly authority,
disappear: they belong to the heavenly realm; all that

remains is a pointer to a word that has been done. By God, of course. Just as it is God who made it known to them through the angels.

So they set off, heaven behind them, and the earthly sign before them. But, Lord, what a sign! Not even the Child, but a child. Some child or other. No special child. Not a child radiating a light of glory, as the religious painters depicted, but on the contrary: a child that looks as inglorious as possible. Wrapped in swaddling clothes. So that it cannot move. It lies there, imprisoned, as it were, in the clothes in which it has been wrapped through the solicitude of others. There is nothing elevating about the manger in which it lies, either, nothing even remotely corresponding to the heavenly glory of the singing angels. There is practically nothing even half worth seeing; the destination of the shepherds' nightly journey is the most ordinary scene. Indeed, in its poverty it is decidedly disappointing. It is something entirely human and ordinary, something quite profane, in no way distinguished—except for the fact that this is the promised sign, and it fits.

The shepherds believe the word. The word sends them from heaven and to earth, and as they proceed along this path, from light to darkness, from the extraordinary to the ordinary, from the solitary experience of God to the realm of ordinary human intercourse, from the splendor above to the poverty below, they are given the confirmation they need: the sign fits. Only now does their fearful joy under heaven's radiance turn into a completely uninhibited, human and Christian joy. Because it fits. And why does it fit? Because the Lord, the High God, has taken the same path as they have: he has left his glory behind him and gone into the dark world, into the child's apparent insignificance, into the unfreedom of human restrictions and bonds, into the poverty of the crib. This is the Word in action, and as yet the shepherds do not know, no one knows, how far down into the darkness this Word-in-action will lead. At all events it will descend much deeper than anyone else into what is worldly, apparently insignificant and profane; into what is bound, poor and powerless; so much so that we shall not be able to follow the last stage of his path. A heavy stone will block the way, preventing the others from approaching, while, in utter night, in ultimate loneliness and forsakenness, he descends to his dead human brothers.

It is true, therefore: in order that he shall find God,

the Christian is placed on the streets of the world, sent to his manacled and poor brethren, to all who suffer, hunger and thirst; to all who are naked, sick and in prison. From henceforth this is his place; he must identify with them all. This is the great joy that is proclaimed to him today, for it is the same way that God sent a Savior to us. We ourselves may be poor and in bondage too, in need of liberation; yet at the same time all of us who have been given a share in the joy of deliverance are sent to be companions of those who are poor and in bondage.

But who will step out along this road that leads from God's glory to the figure of the poor Child lying in the manger? Not the person who is taking a walk for his own pleasure. He will walk along other paths that are more likely to run in the opposite direction, paths that lead from the misery of his own existence toward some imaginary or dreamed-up attempt at a heaven, whether of a brief pleasure or of a long oblivion. The only one to journey from heaven, through the world, to the hell of the lost, is he who is aware, deep in his heart, of a mission to do so; such a one obeys a call that is stronger than his own comfort and his resistance. This is a call that has complete power and authority over my life; I submit to it because it comes from a higher plane than my entire existence. It is an appeal to my heart, demanding the investment of my total self; its hidden, magisterial radiance obliges me, willy-nilly, to submit. I may not know who it is that so takes me into his service. But one thing I do know: if I stay locked within myself, if I seek myself, I shall not find the peace that is promised to the man on whom God's favor rests. I must go. I must enter the service of the poor and imprisoned. I must lose my soul if I am to regain it, for so long as I hold onto it, I shall lose it. This implacable, silent word (which yet is so unmistakable) burns in my heart and will not leave me in peace.

In other lands there are millions who are starving, who work themselves to death for a derisory day's wage, heartlessly exploited like cattle. There too are the slaughtered peoples whose wars cannot end because certain interests (which are not theirs) are tied up with the continuance of their misery. And I know that all my talk about progress and mankind's liberation will be dismissed with laughter and mockery by all the realistic forecasters of mankind's next few decades. Indeed, I only need to open my eyes and ears, and I shall hear the cry of those unjustly oppressed growing louder every day, along with the clamor of those who are resolved to gain power at any price, through hatred and annihilation. These are the superpowers of darkness; in the face of them all our courage drains away, and we lose all belief in the mission that resides in our hearts, that mission that was once so bright, joyous and peace bringing; we lose all hope of really finding the poor Child wrapped in swaddling clothes. What can my pitiful mission achieve, this drop of water in the white-hot furnace? What is the point of my efforts, my dedication, my sacrifice, my pleading to God for a world that is resolved to perish?

"Be not afraid; for behold, I bring you Good News of a great joy. . . . This day is born the Savior," that is, he who, as Son of God and Son of the Father, has traveled (in obedience to the Father) the path that leads away from the Father and into the darkness of the world. Behind him omnipotence and freedom; before, powerlessness, bonds and obedience. Behind him the comprehensive divine vision; before him the prospect of the meaninglessness of death on the Cross between two criminals. Behind him the bliss of life with the Father; before him, grievous solidarity with all who do not know the Father, do not want to know him and deny his existence. Rejoice then, for God himself has passed this way! The Son took with him the awareness of doing the Father's will. He took with him the unceasing prayer that the Father's will would be done on the dark earth as in the brightness of heaven. He took with him his rejoicing that the Father had hidden these things from the wise and revealed them to babes, to the simple and the poor. "I am the way," and this way is "the truth" for you; along this way you will find "the life." Along "the way" that I am you will learn to lose your life in order to find it; you will learn to grow beyond yourselves and your insincerity into a truth that is greater than you are. From a worldly point of view everything may seem very dark; your dedication may seem unproductive and a failure. But do not be afraid: you are on God's path. "Let not your hearts be troubled. believe in God; believe also in me." I am walking on ahead of you and blazing the trail of Christian love for you. It leads to your most inaccessible brother, the person most forsaken by God. But it is the path of divine love itself. You are on the right path. All who deny themselves in order to carry out love's commission are on the right path.

Miracles happen along this path. Apparently

insignificant miracles, noticed by hardly anyone. The very finding of a Child wrapped in swaddling clothes, lying in a manger—is this not a miracle in itself? Then there is the miracle when a particular mission, hidden in a person's heart, really reaches its goal, bringing God's peace and joy where there were nothing but despair and resignation; when someone succeeds in striking a tiny light in the midst of an overpowering darkness. When joy irradiates a heart that no longer dared to believe in it. Now and again we ourselves are assured that the angel's word we are trying to obey will bring us to the place where God's Word and Son is already made man. We are assured that, in spite of all the noise and nonsense, December 25 is Christmas just as truly as two millennia ago. Once and for all God has started out on his journey toward us, and nothing, till the world's end, will stop him from coming to us and abiding in us.

Christmas Poem

Mary Oliver

Says a country legend told every year:
Go to the barn on Christmas Eve and see
what the creatures do as that long night tips over.
Down on their knees they will go, the fire
of an old memory whistling through their minds!

I went. Wrapped to my eyes against the cold
I creaked back the barn door and peered in.
From town the church bells spilled their midnight
music,
and the beasts listened—
yet they lay in their stalls like stone.

GOODNESS AND LIGHT

Oh the heretics!
Not to remember Bethlehem,
or the star as bright as a sun,
or the child born on a bed of straw!
To know only of the dissolving Now!

Still they drowsed on —
citizens of the pure, the physical world,
they loomed in the dark: powerful
of body, peaceful of mind,
innocent of history.

Brothers! I whispered. *It is Christmas!*
And you are no heretics, but a miracle,
immaculate still as when you thundered forth
on the morning of creation!
As for Bethlehem, that blazing star

still sailed the dark, but only looked for me.
Caught in its light, listening again to its story,
I curled against some sleepy beast, who nuzzled
my hair as though I were a child, and warmed me
the best it could all night.

↝

Christmas Eve Vigil

Kathleen Norris

A woman I know, whose family owns a retail business in a small town, once commented, "Christmas is not a pleasant time at our house." I found this a sad commentary on what Christmas has become for so many of us: a time of increased anxiety and stress and discord. We lash out at loved ones because we're spending money we can't afford to spend, or, as with this woman, because Christmas is what makes or breaks our family's livelihood for the year.

What a mess we have made of God's greatest gift to us! We scurry for weeks, baking, shopping, working extra hours, rehearsing and presenting Christmas pageants. Then, on the eve of the Nativity, we force our frantic, over-stimulated children into their "best," most uncomfortable clothes, and we all rush off to church where we collapse into a pew. If we're lucky, we think, we can nod off listening to the lengthy recitation of Jesus' genealogy that opens the Gospel of Matthew. After that, it's playing Santa, and confronting those maddening "some assembly required" directions until the wee hours.

By Christmas Eve, most of us find ourselves very far from our true reasons for celebrating, reasons that are so eloquently expressed in the processional of the Christmas Vigil in the Byzantine rite: "Rejoice, Jerusalem! All you lovers of Sion, share our festivities! On this day the age-old bonds of Adam's condemnation were broken, paradise was opened for us, the serpent was crushed, and the woman, whom he once deceived, lives now as mother of the creator."

Here, in just a few simple words, is the essence of Christmas. It is not merely the birth of Jesus we celebrate tonight, although we recall it joyfully, in song and story. The feast of the Incarnation invites us to celebrate also Jesus' death, resurrection, and coming again in glory. It is our salvation story, and all of creation is invited to dance, sing, and feast. But we are so exhausted. How is it possible to bridge the gap between our sorry reality and the glad, grateful recognition of the Incarnation as the mainstay of our faith? We might begin by acknowledging that if we have neglected the spiritual call of Advent for yet another year, and have allowed ourselves to become thoroughly frazzled by December 24, all is not lost. We are, in fact, in very good shape for Christmas.

It is precisely because we are weary, and poor in spirit, that God can touch us with hope. This is not an easy truth. It means that we accept our common lot, and take up our share of the cross. It means that we do not gloss over the evils we confront every day, both within ourselves and without. Our sacrifices may be great. But as the martyred archbishop of El Salvador, Oscar Romero, once said, it is only the poor and hungry, those who know they need someone to come on their behalf, who can celebrate Christmas.

Tonight we are asked to acknowledge that the world we have made is in darkness. We are asked to be attentive, and keep vigil for the light of Christ. The readings are not particularly comforting. Psalm 88, a lament which is also commonly read on Good Friday, is stark in its appraisal: "For my soul is full of troubles, and my life draws near to Sheol," the underworld of the dead. The passage from Acts asks us to consider that, just as Israel needed God to lead them out of Egypt, so we need Christ to lead us out of our present slavery to sin. We, and our world, are broken. Even our homes have become places of physical and psychological violence. It is only God, through Jesus Christ, who can make us whole again.

The prophecy of Isaiah allows us to imagine a time when God's promise will be fulfilled, and we will no longer be desolate, or forsaken, but found, and beloved of God. We find a note of hope also in the Gospel of Matthew. In the long list of Jesus' forbears, we find the whole range of humanity: not only God's faithful, but adulterers, murderers, rebels, conspirators, transgressors of all sorts, both the fearful and the bold. And yet God's purpose is not thwarted. In Jesus Christ, God turns even human dysfunction to the good.

The genealogy of Jesus reveals that God chooses to work with us as we are, using our weaknesses, even more than our strengths, to fulfill the divine purpose. At tonight's vigil, in a world as cold and cruel and unjust as it was at the time of Jesus' birth in a stable, we desire something better. And in desiring it, we come to believe that it is possible. We await its coming in hope.

Prayer

O God, who spoke all creation into being:
When you created human flesh,
we betrayed you by our disobedience.
When you led us out of slavery in Egypt,
we doubted and defied you.
Yet you chose to come among us
through your Son, Jesus Christ,
who suffered death on our behalf,
putting an end to the power of sin and death.
For this great gift of your steadfast hope,
we give you thanks.
Help us, O Lord, to keep vigil this night.
Help us to watch for the signs of your coming into our
midst,
not in the splendid palaces of power,
but in hearts humbled by need.
Help us to believe that the darkness of cruelty and sin
will never overcome the light, and the mercy, of Christ.
Help us to endure,
knowing that the evil and injustice of this world
cannot prevail against your Word.
We ask this in the name of your Word made flesh,
our Savior, Jesus Christ. Amen.

A Burst of Brilliant Light

Pope Francis

*The people who walked in darkness have
seen a great light.* —Isaiah 9:1

This prophecy of Isaiah never ceases to touch us, especially when we hear it proclaimed in the liturgy of Christmas Night. This is not simply an emotional or sentimental matter. It moves us because it states the deep reality of what we are: a people who walk, and all around us—and within us as well—there is darkness and light. In this night, as the spirit of darkness enfolds the world, there takes place anew the event which always amazes and surprises us: the people who walk see a great light. A light which makes us reflect on this mystery: the mystery of *walking* and *seeing*.

Walking. This verb makes us reflect on the course

of history, that long journey which is the history of salvation, starting with Abraham, our father in faith, whom the Lord called one day to set out, to go forth from his country towards the land which he would show him. From that time on, our identity as believers has been that of a people making its pilgrim way towards the promised land. This history has always been accompanied by the Lord! He is ever faithful to his covenant and to his promises. Because he is faithful, "God is light, and in him there is no darkness at all" (1 John 1:5). Yet on the part of the people there are times of both light and darkness, fidelity and infidelity, obedience, and rebellion; times of being a pilgrim people and times of being a people adrift.

In our personal history too, there are both bright and dark moments, lights and shadows. If we love God and our brothers and sisters, we walk in the light; but if our heart is closed, if we are dominated by pride, deceit, self-seeking, then darkness falls within us and around us. "Whoever hates his brother—writes the Apostle John—is in the darkness; he walks in the darkness, and does not know the way to go, because the darkness has blinded his eyes" (1 John 2:11). A people who walk, but as a pilgrim people who do not want to go astray.

On this night, like a burst of brilliant light, there rings out the proclamation of the Apostle: "God's grace has been revealed, and it has made salvation possible for the whole human race" (Titus 2:11).

The grace which was revealed in our world is Jesus, born of the Virgin Mary, true man and true God. He has entered our history; he has shared our journey. He came to free us from darkness and to grant us light. In him was revealed the grace, the mercy, and the tender love of the Father: Jesus is Love incarnate. He is not simply a teacher of wisdom, he is not an ideal for which we strive while knowing that we are hopelessly distant from it. He is the meaning of life and history, who has pitched his tent in our midst.

The shepherds were the first to see this "tent," to receive the news of Jesus' birth. They were the first because they were among the last, the outcast. And they were the first because they were awake, keeping watch in the night, guarding their flocks. The pilgrim is bound by duty to keep watch and the shepherds did just that. Together with them, let us pause before the Child, let us pause in silence. Together with them, let us thank the Lord for having given Jesus to us, and with them let us raise from the depths of our hearts the praises of his fidelity: We bless you, Lord God most high, who lowered yourself for our sake. You are immense, and you made yourself small; you are rich and you made yourself poor; you are all-powerful and you made yourself vulnerable.

On this night let us share the *joy of the Gospel*: God loves us, he so loves us that he gave us his Son to be our brother, to be light in our darkness. To us the Lord repeats: "Do not be afraid!" (Luke 2:10). As the angels said to the shepherds: "Do not be afraid!". And I also repeat to all of you: Do not be afraid! Our Father is patient, he loves us, he gives us Jesus to guide us on the way which leads to the promised land. Jesus is the light who brightens the darkness. He is mercy: our Father always forgives us. He is our peace. Amen.

~~

Have a Defiant Christmas!

John Shea

In those long ago days of Christmas innocence when it always snowed gently in a starry and windless night, my parents would hustle my sisters and me into the back seat of the car. We would drive slowly, snow crunching under cold tires, into the neighborhoods of the rich to see the "lights."

The "lights" were decorations that people put up on the outside of their houses and lawns. Multicolored lights would be strung over an entire house, etching door-frames and windows, wrapped round into wreaths and bows. In the frozen front yard there were figures of cardboard and plastic, even stone, ranging in size from a small child to an overgrown adult. They were the usual suspects, a mix of *The Night*

Before Christmas and the Crib—reindeer and wise men, sleighs and shepherds, elves and Mary, angels and carolers, Santa Claus and Baby Jesus. Occasionally, the stiff, on-guard soldiers from the Nutcracker Suite would make an appearance. All were lit up so that night passengers in slow moving cars could gawk through frosted windows and say, "Look at that one!"

But it was not these sprawling scenes that first welcomed me into the truth of Christmas. It was my own decorated home, seen in a new way.

One Christmas when we returned from our trip to see the "lights," I pushed out of the back seat, straightened up, and saw our house, as if for the first time. We lived in a two-flat. My grandparents lived on the first floor; and since they usually went to bed around nine (a custom I have recently begun to imitate), their flat was dark. Our flat on the second floor was also dark —except for the Christmas tree.

The tree was strung with lights, and their soft glow could be seen through the upper window. The outer darkness was all around, yet the tree shone in the darkness. There was no razzle-dazzle, no blinking on and off, no glitz, no "Oh, wow!" There was just a steady shining, a simple juxtaposition of light and darkness. Its beauty drew me.

I ran up the stairs. My parents had already un-locked the door and turned on the house lights. I sat in a chair and stayed with the tree. The attraction of the tree continued for a while and then began to recede. Soon the practical took over. I noticed some tinsel that needed to be smoothed and re-hung. As I tinkered with it, whatever was left of the tree's radi-ance dimmed. Then, abruptly, the revelation ceased. It became merely a pine tree shedding needles on the rug.

It was only when I was older that I knew in a men-tal way what my child's heart had intuited. Christmas tries to point to an inner light, a tree of lights inside the house of our being, and invites us to come close and ponder its beauty. We notice this light because it is contrasted with an outer darkness. And it defies this darkness, refusing to allow the outer world to dictate the terms of existence.

Yet it is important to note the darkness does not go away. Although it is not the overwhelming power it pretends to be, darkness plays an essential role in be-coming conscious of the revelation. "What has come into being *in* him was life and the life was the light of all people. The light shines in the darkness, and the darkness did not overcome it" (John 1:4-5).

The Christmas revelation can be phrased: no matter how severe the darkness of the outer world is, it cannot overcome the inner and transcendent light. Although we do not always reflect on it, there is an edge to Christmas, an in-your-face attitude. Chesterton put it simply and well: "A religion that defies the world should have a feast that defies the weather." So I wish you a defiant Christmas.

Of course, I really do not want you to have a defiant Christmas. I want you to have a harmonious Christmas. I want the inner and outer world to be in sync. Light inside and out. In other words, I wish you and all people the full peace of Christmas—good enough health, good enough finances, good enough relationships, and a good enough, stable, non-violent society and world. As the lapel button from the sixties put it, "Parousia Now!" Idealistic as it is, that's what I want for every stumblebum of us.

But that is not what we always get. Christmas arrives to find our health precarious, our careers, jobs, or vocations under stress; our finances dipping badly; our relationships in need of repair; our society and world either slightly or wildly insane. How can we celebrate Christmas in situations like these? Aren't negative circumstances too much for us? Do they not call the shots, either tentatively supporting us or conspiring to break us?

The Christmas answer is: "Give them their due, but not your soul." When the outer world is darkness, Christmas encourages us to rest in the inner world of light and bring that light into the outer world of darkness. Since this inner world is rooted in a transcendent love, it is more powerful than all the attacks that emerge out of both our finitude and sinfulness. "I have said this that you might have peace in me. In the world you have tribulations, but cheer up, I have overcome the world" (John 16:33). Christmas cheer, when it is modeled on this passage from the Gospel of John, engenders in us a gentle defiance toward the tribulations of the world. Gentle defiance is neither negative nor angry. It just manages to find a greater love by which to be held and energized. This capacity for defiance may be the Christmas gift that we will all need to unwrap during one December or another.

The Birth of Jesus

Mary Christine Athans

I had made the journey from Nazareth to Jerusalem many times—usually for Passover. But to make the trip when I was nine months pregnant was something I would never have imagined. The Roman governor was demanding that all males register, and Joseph, because he was of the house and family of David, had to go to Bethlehem —just a short distance from Jerusalem. Such a long and hilly road from Galilee! I was grateful to have the donkey to ride, and Joseph guided it carefully over the rocky road. It took us a little more than four days, and with each day I was sure the baby would be born at any moment.

Joseph had urged me to stay in Nazareth where I would be more comfortable. We had made our preparations for the baby there. But I would not let him go alone, and I did not want to be at a distance from him at such a special time. Besides, I knew he really wanted me to come so that we could be together when the baby was born. We had been through so much together. He had been so loyal and good despite his inability to understand the great mystery. His faithfulness was almost like the faithfulness of God. "I thank you for your faithfulness and love which excel all we ever knew of you. On the day I called, you answered; you increased the strength of my soul" (Psalm 138:2–3). Joseph loved and cared for me when he could so easily have left. How can I ever love and appreciate him enough?

It was late at night when we arrived in Bethlehem, and the little town was filled to overflowing. We tried so hard to find a place to stay. If I were not expecting the baby at any moment we could have been satisfied with any place—even spread out some blankets in a field. But we needed some privacy for the delivery. Finally, an innkeeper named Jacob was sympathetic when he saw I was so very pregnant. Although they had no room, he called his wife, Sarah. She realized I was ready to give birth at any moment and hastened me around to a stable behind the inn where they kept the animals at night.

It was a clean place, and the animals looked peaceful. Sarah immediately made preparations for the birth—brought water and cloths. I don't know what I would have done without her. I am sure she must have assisted others in the past. She knew all the right things to do. It all happened so quickly. By the time Joseph arrived at the stable after having made arrangements with Jacob, the innkeeper, he could hear the crying baby—and he was so overjoyed! It was a beautiful healthy child—a boy, just as I had been told. We breathed a sigh of relief. Sarah cut the umbilical cord, washed the baby, wrapped him in swaddling clothes and put him in my arms. They wanted to know his name, and we said "Jesus." Jacob and Sarah looked on smiling, almost as if he was their grandchild.

They brought us food, but I was too exhausted and excited to eat. Some shepherds nearby must have heard Jesus crying, because they asked if they could come in and see the baby. They were people of the land—the *am ha-uaretz*—simple and joyful. We could hear music nearby as well—although we could not tell if it was from the inn or from travelers going by. It was a very joyful song—with a sense of shalom—heartfelt music that almost brought tears to my eyes. It was peaceful, yet exhilarating, and I was so grateful.

In time, the shepherds left, and the musicians moved on. Sarah and Jacob made excuses that they needed to go in and tend to their guests, but I think they knew we wanted to savor the moment by ourselves. What would we ever have done without them? I was physically and emotionally exhausted but too excited to sleep.

Finally, Joseph and I were alone with this beautiful child. We snuggled down into the straw with the new baby between us. We were both awed by this remarkable gift of life. What can one say at such an ecstatic moment when the heart is so full of joy and gratitude? Suddenly I found myself smiling, and I knew what was in my heart. I said softly, "Joseph, do you think we should say a *She-he-chee-ya-nu?*" He nodded and smiled, and we prayed together,

> *Ba-ruch a-tah A-don-ai*
> *E-lo-hei-nu, me-lech ha-o-lam,*
> *She-he-chee-ya-nu ve-ki-ye-ma-nu*
> *ve-hi-gi-a-nu- la-ze-man ha-zeh.*

> Blessed are You, O Lord our
> God, Ruler of the Universe,
> who has given us life,

and sustained us,
and brought us to this very special
moment.

I can't say for sure that the She-he-chec-ya-nu *would have been said in the first century, but it is very old. The prayer is referenced in the Mishnah. I would not be surprised if, just maybe, that was the prayer that Mary and Joseph said on that very special night.*

Christmas Confession

Anne Rice

I am a Christmas Christian. I always have been. For me, the image that most deeply and significantly reflects the crucial truth of my faith is that of the little Christ child in the Manger, surrounded by his loving parents, the shepherds who have come to pay Him homage, and the three magnificent magi approaching with their precious gifts.

Is there anyone in the Western World who is not familiar with the Christmas iconography, who has not seen some representation somewhere of the Bethlehem tableaux?

Most of us have seen it countless times, on the walls of museums in great paintings, in the greeting cards that arrive in the weeks before Christmas, in the little statues we ourselves place beneath the Christmas tree, oftentimes with a snow covered wooden stable, to remind us that Christ has come into the world again this Christmas Eve.

It's no secret that erudite biblical scholars question the Christmas story. No one knows after all when Our Lord Jesus Christ was born. And many hold that the "fabulous" infancy stories were late additions to the gospels, seeking to make a myth of a birth that is shrouded in obscurity. Some maintain that the placing of this glorious little story in the dead of winter was a shameful attempt to graft the myth of Christ upon the midwinter festivals of a dying paganism through which people had celebrated for centuries the miracle of life surviving the darkest and coldest days of the year.

Is it not beautiful to think on it, the way our ancestors since time immemorial gathered around their great flickering fires, or sat down to banquets of plenty as the winds howled and the snow fell upon roofs and fields, and the sun all but vanished in the shortest days of the year?

Was it a slick move by the early church authorities to celebrate the birth of Christ in the middle of winter, or was it perhaps an accidental stroke of genius that connected the powerful story of Christ's birth to the time of the year when poverty and want are felt most keenly, as Dickens put it, and when people struggle so valiantly to keep the faith that times will be better, that suffering, deprivation, cold, will inevitably come to an end?

There is a season for all things under Heaven and it seems to me that the church chose exactly the right season for the Christ to be born.

The story of the Incarnation is, after all, not like any other. Here we have the greatest inversion perhaps that the world has even seen. In the person of the Christ Child, the Maker of the Universe has come down to be born a helpless infant in our midst.

All who look at the Christmas Crib understand that the Divine Son of God will grow like any other human child, becoming a young boy and later a man, and that His journey with us will last some thirty to thirty-three years before He will die with us, just as we ourselves die. As we all know, His resurrection will then offer us the hope that we too will survive not only the worst of winters but the only supernatural event we can know this side of heaven, the extinguishing of our physical lives.

Is there a more beautiful love story in our literature than that of God coming to be with us, coming to suffer the mundane and vulgar indignities of our physical world?

I do not know of any.

And when I ponder the never-ending journey of Christianity through history, I wonder if it is not the story of the Incarnation that gives the belief system its seemingly eternal power: the single idea that the God who made us is one of us, that God is beyond us yet became human as we are, returning inevitably to Heaven with a body as human as our bodies, even marked in eternity with the wounds of His cruel physical death.

But the genius of the Christmas Crib is that you do not need theology to approach it. You do not need any bloody atonement theory to touch the Christ Child's outstretched hand. The story is complete there without the horror of the cross. Christ has embraced our helplessness. Christ has enshrined our physicality within the limitless power of the Maker of all things.

In a world in which religions alienate and confuse, in which hierarchies struggle with corruption and believers often turn bitterly and in defeat from the warring orthodoxies of Christ's followers, the Christ

Child merely gazes from His bed of hay at all comers, saying quietly:

You are part of me. I am part of you.

I am always and forever here with you.

If "civilization as we know it" were coming to an end with predictable falling bombs and fleeing populations, if we had to clear out of this house with only a handful of possessions for a post-apocalyptic world of ruin and struggle, what would I take with me to preserve for generations yet unborn who might never know the millions of texts we hold to be classics, for whom the pages of the bible might disappear?

I'd take the Christmas creche—the child, his quiet and patient parents, the ragged shepherds with their sheep, the faithful ox and the donkey, the Wise Men in their gilded raiment come to gaze in unquestioning awe.

I'd clutch those little statues to my heart, and hope to leave them somewhere safe where others might inevitably find them—gathered in their ancient configuration—and ponder the mystery of the child's humble birth amid rich and poor, animal and human, snow and straw.

The creche tells the story I believe in more surely than the printed word. And it always will.

Whatever we face, in the physical and emotional winters of our lives, there is always faith that the God who made us will never abandon us, that he will be born again inside each of us, ever ready to help us save ourselves.

Papa Panov's Special Christmas

Leo Tolstoy

It was Christmas Eve and although it was still afternoon, lights had begun to appear in the shops and houses of the little Russian village, for the short winter day was nearly over. Excited children scurried indoors and now only muffled sounds of chatter and laughter escaped from closed shutters.

Old Papa Panov, the village shoemaker, stepped outside his shop to take one last look around. The sounds of happiness, the bright lights and the faint but delicious smells of Christmas cooking reminded him of past Christmas times when his wife had still been alive and his own children little. Now they had gone. His usually cheerful face, with the little laughter wrinkles behind the round steel spectacles, looked sad now. But he went back indoors with a firm step, put up the shutters and set a pot of coffee to heat on the charcoal stove. Then, with a sigh, he settled in his big armchair.

Papa Panov did not often read, but tonight he pulled down the big old family Bible and, slowly tracing the lines with one forefinger, he read again the Christmas story. He read how Mary and Joseph, tired by their journey to Bethlehem, found no room for them at the inn, so that Mary's little baby was born in the cowshed.

"Oh, dear, oh, dear!" exclaimed Papa Panov, "if only they had come here! I would have given them my bed, and I could have covered the baby with my patchwork quilt to keep him warm."

He read on about the wise men who had come to see the baby Jesus, bringing him splendid gifts. Papa Panov's face fell. "I have no gift that I could give him," he thought sadly.

Then his face brightened. He put down the Bible, got up and stretched his long arms to the shelf high up in his little room. He took down a small, dusty box and opened it. Inside was a perfect pair of tiny leather shoes. Papa Panov smiled with satisfaction. Yes, they were as good as he had remembered—the best shoes he had ever made. "I should give him those," he decided, as he gently put them away and sat down again.

He was feeling tired now, and the further he read the sleepier he became. The print began to dance before his eyes so that he closed them, just for a minute. In no time at all Papa Panov was fast asleep.

And as he slept he dreamed. He dreamed that someone was in his room and he knew at once, as one does in dreams, who the person was. It was Jesus.

"You have been wishing that you could see me, Papa Panov," he said kindly, "then look for me tomorrow. It will be Christmas Day, and I will visit you. But look carefully, for I shall not tell you who I am."

When at last Papa Panov awoke, the bells were ringing out and a thin light was filtering through the shutters. "Bless my soul!" said Papa Panov. "It's Christmas Day!"

He stood up and stretched himself, for he was rather stiff. Then his face filled with happiness as he remembered his dream. This would be a very special Christmas after all, for Jesus was coming to visit him. How would he look? Would he be a little baby, as at that first Christmas? Would he be a grown man, a carpenter—or the great King that he is, God's Son?

He must watch carefully the whole day through so that he recognized him however he came.

Papa Panov put on a special pot of coffee for his Christmas breakfast, took down the shutters and looked out of the window. The street was deserted, no one was stirring yet. No one except the road sweeper. He looked as miserable and dirty as ever, and well he might! Whoever wanted to work on Christmas Day—and in the raw cold and bitter freezing mist of such a morning?

Papa Panov opened the shop door, letting in a thin stream of cold air. "Come in!" he shouted across the street cheerily. "Come in and have some hot coffee to keep out the cold!"

The sweeper looked up, scarcely able to believe his ears. He was only too glad to put down his broom and come into the warm room. His old clothes steamed gently in the heat of the stove and he clasped both red hands round the comforting warm mug as he drank.

Papa Panov watched him with satisfaction, but every now and then his eyes strayed to the window. It would never do to miss his special visitor.

"Expecting someone?" the sweeper asked at last. So Papa Panov told him about his dream.

"Well, I hope he comes," the sweeper said, "you've

given me a bit of Christmas cheer I never expected to have. I'd say you deserve to have your dream come true." And he actually smiled.

When he had gone, Papa Panov put on cabbage soup for his dinner, then went to the door again, scanning the street. He saw no one. But he was mistaken. Someone was coming.

The girl walked so slowly and quietly, hugging the walls of shops and houses, that it was a while before he noticed her. She looked very tired and she was carrying something. As she drew nearer he could see that it was a baby, wrapped in a thin shawl. There was such sadness in her face and in the pinched little face of the baby, that Papa Panov's heart went out to them.

"Won't you come in," he called, stepping outside to meet them. "You both need a warm by the fire and a rest."

The young mother let him shepherd her indoors and to the comfort of the armchair. She gave a big sigh of relief.

"I'll warm some milk for the baby," Papa Panov said, "I've had children of my own—I can feed her for you." He took the milk from the stove and carefully fed the baby from a spoon, warming her tiny feet by the stove at the same time.

"She needs shoes," the cobbler said.

But the girl replied, "I can't afford shoes, I've got no husband to bring home money. I'm on my way to the next village to get work."

Sudden thought flashed through Papa Panov's mind. He remembered the little shoes he had looked at last night. But he had been keeping those for Jesus. He looked again at the cold little feet and made up his mind.

"Try these on her," he said, handing the baby and the shoes to the mother. The beautiful little shoes were a perfect fit. The girl smiled happily and the baby gurgled with pleasure.

"You have been so kind to us," the girl said, when she got up with her baby to go. "May all your Christmas wishes come true!"

But Papa Panov was beginning to wonder if his very special Christmas wish would come true. Perhaps he had missed his visitor? He looked anxiously up and down the street. There were plenty of people about but they were all faces that he recognized. There were neighbors going to call on their families. They nodded and smiled and wished him Happy Christmas! Or beggars—and Papa Panov hurried indoors to fetch them hot soup and a generous hunk of bread, hurrying out again in case he missed the Important Stranger.

All too soon the winter dusk fell. When Papa Panov next went to the door and strained his eyes, he could no longer make out the passers-by. Most were home and indoors by now anyway. He walked slowly back into his room at last, put up the shutters, and sat down wearily in his armchair.

So it had been just a dream after all. Jesus had not come.

Then all at once he knew that he was no longer alone in the room.

This was not dream for he was wide awake. At first he seemed to see before his eyes the long stream of people who had come to him that day. He saw again the old road sweeper, the young mother and her baby, and the beggars he had fed. As they passed, each whispered, "Didn't you see me, Papa Panov?"

"Who are you?" he called out, bewildered.

Then another voice answered him. It was the voice from his dream—the voice of Jesus.

"I was hungry and you fed me," he said. "I was naked and you clothed me. I was cold and you warmed me. I came to you today in every one of those you helped and welcomed."

Then all was quiet and still. Only the sound of the big clock ticking. A great peace and happiness seemed to fill the room, overflowing Papa Panov's heart until he wanted to burst out singing and laughing and dancing with joy.

"So he did come after all!" was all that he said.

Holy Innocents

Robert Ellsberg

Rise, take the child and his mother, and flee to Egypt and remain there till I tell you; for Herod is about to search for the child, to destroy him.
—MATTHEW 2:13

It is the constant fear of every tyrant that somewhere, perhaps in an obscure village, perhaps at that very moment, there is a baby born who will one day signal the end of his power. According to the Gospel of Matthew, this fear was realized for King Herod when wandering wise men from the East came to Jerusalem asking, "Where is he who has been born king of the Jews?"

By all accounts, Herod was a man of extreme brutality. He conceived of a simple plan: Rather than sit and wait anxiously for the day of reckoning with this future "king," why not simply kill the babe before he could grow and pose a threat? But when the wise men failed to cooperate with his plan, Herod simply ordered his troops to the village of Bethlehem, there to kill every male child under the age of two. The order was given, and it was dutifully carried out.

But the reader knows, as Herod does not, that the massacre is pointless. Joseph, forewarned in a dream, has taken his family into exile in Egypt. The child lives.

This terrible story, omitted from the typical Christmas pageant, is a vivid reminder of the violent world into which Jesus was born. There were certainly those for whom the coming of the Messiah represented anything but good news. Did Jesus at some point learn the story of his birth and of the children who had perished in his place? If so, that chapter in his education is reserved for his "hidden years," beyond the scope of the Gospel narratives. From the early centuries, however, the church has commemorated the feast of these Holy Innocents. Unlike traditional martyrs who would later die bearing witness to Christ, these little ones died unwittingly in the place of Christ. They were killed by the same interests that would later conspire in the death of Jesus and for the same reasons—to stifle from birth any hope that the world might be changed.

In our own time whole villages have been massacred on the basis of similar reports: "In such-and-such-a-hamlet the peasants have formed a cooperative. . . . It is said that in such-a-village poor families are gathering at night to read the Bible and other subversive literature. . . . It is well known where this is likely to lead. . . . Advise that appropriate action be taken before the danger spreads."

The feast of the Holy Innocents is not simply a memorial to those who died before their time. These infants represent all those cut down to prevent the seed of liberation from taking root and growing. They are those who die in the dream of a different future, hoping but never knowing that their redeemer lives. In remembering the feast of the Holy Innocents the church commemorates these victims of Herod's rage. But it also celebrates his failure.

His power is doomed. The child lives.

Jesus the Worker

Walter J. Ciszek, SJ

There was the realization that work of itself is not a curse, but a sharing in God's own work of creation, a redemptive and redeeming act, noble of itself and worthy of the best in man—even as it was worthy of God himself.

There is a tremendous truth contained in the realization that when God became man he became a workingman. Not a king, not a chieftain, not a warrior or a statesman or a great leader of nations, as some had thought the Messiah would be. The Gospels show us Christ the teacher, the healer, the wonderworker, but these activities of his public life were the work of three short years. For the rest of the time of his life on earth, God was a village carpenter and the son of a carpenter. He did not fashion benches or tables or beds or roof beams or plowbeams by means of miracles, but by hammer and saw, by ax and adz. He worked long hours to help his father, and then became the support of his widowed mother, by the rough work of a hill country craftsman. Nothing he worked on, as far as we know, ever set any fashions or became a collector's item. He worked in a shop every day, week in and week out, for some twenty years. He did the work all of us have to do in our lifetimes. There was nothing spectacular about it, there was much of the routine about it, perhaps much that was boring. There is little we can say about the jobs we do or have done that could not be said of the work God himself did when he became a man.

Christmas for Mystics

Marianne Williamson

The holidays are only holy if we make them so.

Otherwise, the assault of modernity—from crass consumerism to a twenty-four-hour news cycle to the compulsivity of the wired world—wrecks whatever we have left of our nervous systems, making the true spiritual meaning of Christmas seem as distant as the furthest star. It's only when we consciously carve out a space for the holy—in our heads, our hearts and our lifestyles—that the deeper mysteries of the season can reveal themselves.

The holidays are a time of spiritual preparation, if we allow them to be. We're preparing for the birth of our possible selves, the event with which we have been psychologically pregnant all our lives. And the labor doesn't happen in our fancy places; there is never "room in the Inn," or room in the intellect, for the birth of our authentic selves. That happens in the manger of our most humble places, with lots of angels, i.e., thoughts of God, all around.

Something happens in that quiet place, where we're simply alone and listening to nothing but our hearts. It's not loneliness, that aloneness. It's rather the solitude of the soul, where we are grounded more deeply in our own internal depths. Then, having connected more deeply to God, we're able to connect more deeply with each other. Our connection to the divine unlocks our connection to the universe.

According to the mystical tradition, Christ is born into the world through each of us. As we open our hearts, he is born into the world. As we choose to forgive, he is born into the world. As we rise to the occasion, he is born into the world. As we make our hearts true conduits for love, and our minds true conduits for higher thoughts, then absolutely a divine birth takes place. Who we're capable of being emerges into the world, and weaknesses of the former self begin to fade. Thus are the spiritual mysteries of the universe, the constant process of dying to who we used to be as we actualize our divine potential.

We make moment-by-moment decisions what kind of people to be—whether to be someone who blesses, or who blames; someone who obsesses about past and future, or who dwells fully in the present; someone who whines about problems, or who creates solutions. It's always our choice what attitudinal ground to stand on: the emotional quicksand of negative thinking, or the airstrip of spiritual flight.

Such choices are made in every moment, consciously or unconsciously, throughout the year. But this is the season when we consider the possibility that we could achieve a higher state of consciousness, not just sometimes but all the time. We consider that there has been one—and the mystical tradition says there have also been others—who so embodied his own divine spark that he is now as an elder brother to us, assigned the task of helping the rest of us do the same. According to *A Course in Miracles*, he doesn't have anything we don't have; he simply doesn't have anything else. He is in a state that is still potential in the rest of us. The image of Jesus has been so perverted, so twisted by institutions claiming to represent him. As stated in the *Course*, "Some bitter idols have been made of him who came only to be brother to the world." But beyond the mythmaking, doctrine and dogma, he is a magnificent spiritual force. And one doesn't have to be Christian to appreciate that fact, or to fall on our knees with praise and thanks at the realization of its meaning. Jesus gives to Christmas its spiritual intensity, hidden behind the ego's lure into all the wild and cacophonous sounds of the season. Beyond the nativity scenes, beyond the doctrinal hoopla, lies one important thing: the hope that we might yet become, while still on this earth, who we truly are.

Then we, and the entire world, will know peace.

◁▷

In Congo or in Croydon, God Is There for Us

Rowan Williams

A thirteen-year-old boy is abducted from his home and for ten years forced to live and work with a gang of violent terrorists. To save his own life, he has to go along with atrocities. He will be brutalized and he will brutalize others. He will have to get used to killing—sometimes killing people he knows. He will be aware that return home is practically unthinkable, because he will be regarded as beyond redemption by most of his neighbors, even his family. He knows that there is nothing in front of him except the likelihood of an early death—a knowledge that he tries to blot out with the drugs that keep him more or less anaesthetized for a lot of the time from the reality of what he has to do.

In June of this year, I had the privilege of spending an evening with about thirty young men and women who had been through this nightmare experience. I met them in Bunia, in Eastern Congo; thirty or so youngsters, none more than the middle twenties, out of several hundred thousand across the globe who have been forced into becoming child soldiers.

I won't try and make readers wince with the details, though they are the sort of thing that you wish you could forget; the important thing is that they had escaped. They had been brought out of the bush, prised out of the grip of the militias that had captured them and reintroduced to something like normality. At twenty-one or twenty-two, some were completing their secondary school work. All had been assured of a safe place to live if they managed to get away from the militias. Many had been reunited with families. They had advocates and helpers in their communities, people who were willing to stick their necks out to support them when others looked at them with suspicion or even disgust.

How had it happened? They all had one answer. The church had not given up on them. At great risk, members of local Christian communities had kept contact with them, sometimes literally gone in search of them, helped them escape and organized a return to civilian life. They had prepared congregations to receive them, love them and gradually get them back into ordinary human relationships.

It wasn't just a story of happy endings. The trauma of these experiences doesn't go away overnight. Drug use, conditioned behavior, the deadening of emotions, all these take time and involve a fair number of failures as well as successes. The miracle is that any manage rehabilitation or perhaps the miracle is that anyone believes enough in the possibility of it.

Yet the message was always the same: "they didn't give up on us."

At Christmas— and at of all times of the year— we need reminding, believers and unbelievers alike, of what sort of difference can be made to the world because of that birth in Bethlehem. Not only can be made, but is made: whether in Congo or in the back streets of our country, plenty of people know that it's only because of those who believe the Christmas message that they have recovered hope for their lives.

And the message is that God has told us he is not going to give up on us: he appears to us in the life of Jesus, a life of complete identification with human suffering and need. And he makes it possible for us to identify in the same way with those who suffer and live in hopelessness and need. He makes it possible not to give up, even where there seems least chance of change.

Last summer, we watched in disbelief and alarm as disorder spread throughout many of our cities. People were swept up in chaos—arson, looting, threats and violence. The majority of people, as usual, were just baffled and angry, desperately wondering what could be done to put things straight again and to show that their communities could still work after all. Remember one of the real miracles of those days—when Tariq Jahan appealed for restraint after the killing of his son.

And one of the stories that hasn't yet been properly told from last summer is how often it was local clergy and local congregations who stepped up to the plate to respond to these longings to do something constructive. These were the folk who turned out to put themselves at the service of all that was best in communities. These were the people who were trusted to broker deals that let emergency services through where they were needed, to set up makeshift support centers offering refreshments. These were the people who were relied on to pick up the pieces in any number of ways. They could do it because they were trusted. And they were trusted because local communities knew they were not going to go away and give up.

"I'm not going away" is one of the most important things we can ever hear, whether we hear it from someone at our bedside in illness or over a shared drink at a time of depression or stress—or at a moment when we wonder what's happening to our neighborhood and our society. This is the heart of what Christmas says about God. And it's the real justification for any local church or any national church being there. When people are pushed by all sorts of destructive forces into seeing themselves as hopeless, as rubbish, so that what they do doesn't matter anymore, it's this that will make the change that matters.

Happy Christmas to you all; and remember when you can the people who think the world has forgotten them—the child soldiers in Congo and elsewhere who haven't yet escaped into the arms of a loving community, the men and women who sit in their rooms or houses in depression and loneliness, the elderly who feel that the world has left them behind and that their feelings and needs don't matter to anyone any longer,

the refugee who has left behind a horrifyingly trau-
matic situation of rape and murder, yet who knows
that he or she is looked on with suspicion and hostil-
ity in their new home. . . . So many. You'll be able to
think of many more, I'm sure.

Pray that they will find that someone hasn't forgotten—that they will find out that God and the friends
of God are there for them.

Amazing Peace

Maya Angelou

It is the Glad Season.

Hope is born again in the faces of children
It rides on the shoulders of our aged as they walk into
their sunsets.
Hope spreads around the earth. Brightening all things,
Even hate which crouches breeding in dark corridors.

In our joy, we think we hear a whisper.
At first it is too soft. Then only half heard.
We listen carefully as it gathers strength.
We hear a sweetness.
The word is Peace.
It is loud now.
Louder than the explosion of bombs.

~≈>

The Shepherds of Bethlehem

Ernesto Cardenal

Near Bethlehem there were some shepherds who were spending the night in the field, watching over their sheep. Suddenly an angel of the Lord appeared, and the glory of the Lord shone round them: and they were very frightened. But the angel said to them, "Don't be afraid, for I bring you good news that will be cause for much joy for all."

We were gathered in the little church. The first to speak was old TOMAS PEÑA, with his customary wonderful simplicity: "The way I see it is that those guys who were watching over their sheep heard good news. There they were just like us here, and they heard good news. Like when we heard that you were coming. They told us that a priest was coming and we couldn't believe it at first, because no priest ever used to come here. . . . Well, it was like this when they were watching over their sheep and they heard good news. They were sad before. They weren't at a party. They were just screwed up."

"And why were they the ones to get the good news?" I asked.

TOMAS PEÑA: "Because they were closer to God. Others were thinking about bad things, and not good things. That's how it seems to me."

PATRICIO: "They were closer to God because they were there at night keeping watch, and since they were keeping watch God wanted to send them good news. It seems to me that that's the way it might have been."

FELIPE: "The angel came to them because they were working men, and I find this is very important for us. Because they were poor little people who were working. They were watching over their sheep which is like taking care of cattle today. They were workers, laborers, poor people. The angel of God could have gone to the king's palace and said to him: 'The Savior has been born.' But the angel didn't go where the king was but where the poor people were, which means that this message is not for the big shots but for the poor little guys, which means the oppressed, which means us."

I: "It was really the shepherds who were at the bottom of the social scale in Israel . . ."

ALEJANDRO: "And the good news is that they're going to find somebody just like themselves, a poor guy wrapped in swaddling clothes."

Today was born in the city of David a Savior for you, who is Christ the Lord.

FELIX: "He's making it clear that it's for them that he's coming. It seems to me that they were like slaves and when they heard that a liberator was coming they were filled with joy. They already knew that a Messiah was coming, and when they hear the angel announce that he's already here they're filled with joy. They know that this birth was going to free them from slavery, because, like the slaves that they were, they were forced to work. A liberator from all slavery. He was coming to liberate all slaves, all poor people, not just poor people of that time but those of today too! Every poor person who lives working for the rich lives like a slave."

FELIPE: "Every worker is always poor, even if he works in a factory."

FELIX goes on: "He was coming to liberate the poor. He wasn't coming to liberate the rich. That's why the news had to come to poor people. It was for them most of all. And it's the same now: The news, the word of God always goes to the poor people. Because I believe that the poor people, because of their poverty, always hear the word of God more often than the rich. A lot of rich people go to church on Sunday but they don't listen to the word of God, they go to enjoy themselves . . . or they don't go."

SABINO: "It's the same with a lot of poor people here. . . . They don't come to church. . . ."

FRANCISCO: "Even the angel didn't reach all the poor people. . . ."

FELIPE: "The Gospel says he came to people who were working, not to people who were loafing."

FELIX: "Well, the Holy Spirit always comes more to poor people nowadays, because the poor people in their slavery have to turn to God every day. And when you least expect it, maybe working in the field, suddenly you get a good idea: That means the Spirit came to you."

OSCAR: "They were like us, poor and in need of a liberator. Because they took care of the animals, but on the other hand they were alone, abandoned by everybody. That's the way we are, humiliated by the rich too. But if somebody comes to tell us that we shouldn't be always serving those rich people like slaves, comes to talk to us about Revolution, something like that, then we gradually realize that we too can struggle."

Julio: "It seems to me that we are the shepherds of the rich people because we work for them. We support them with our work, and a liberator has to come to help us too. We are campesinos and woodcutters, but it seems to me that we don't need an angel to come to tell us personally. Or maybe he already came. . . ."

Felipe: "The angel is any idea, any inspiration that you get in the woods when you're there cutting wood, like Felix says, any idea about doing something for other people, for the community. It's the Holy Spirit, because the Spirit is the spirit of love for others, right?"

Julio: "Well, that's why I just said that maybe that angel already came and we don't need to wait for him to come in the form of a vision, personally, because maybe right now when we're reading this and hearing these words the angel is coming to give us the news."

I: "That's right. At this very moment you are receiving the same news from the angel that the shepherds received."

Laureano: "We already got the news. But we have to do the work. . . ."

"We have to spread the news," interrupted his cousin Julio.

Laureano continued: "To find ways to liberate

ourselves. Because liberation comes through people."

FELIPE: "Those who are against it, it's always because of selfishness."

OSCAR: "Also because of fear. A lot of us are afraid. Afraid that they'll do us some harm, prison, death. . . . And a lot of times this fear is from ignorance."

And as a sign, you will find the baby wrapped in swaddling clothes, lying in a manger.

OSCAR: "He was born in a farmyard. He came for the sake of poor people, the liberator. That's why he had to be born like that. He had to set an example for us. That nobody should think he's better than others. To feel ourselves all the same, equal. Because everybody was born from the same womb, his mother's."

ANGEL, Felix's son: "If they'd been offered a good house wouldn't Mary and Joseph have accepted it?"

RAFAEL: "They wouldn't have turned it down, I bet."

OSCAR: "Then it would have been better if he hadn't come."

FELIX: "He was coming to let the poor know he was their comrade."

ANGEL: "The only reason they didn't accept a house is because nobody offered them one."

JULIO: "Why didn't anybody offer them one?"

Oscar: "They were very poor. That's why."

Tomas Peña: "Maybe people thought they were slippery characters, that they were going to steal. . . ."

Felix: "That's what happens nowadays. If some raggedy people come to the city and ask for a place to stay they don't get any, or if they do it'll be off in a chicken coop, to sleep with the chickens."

Tomas: "If he had been born in a rich man's house the shepherds wouldn't have been able to get there, because it was a fancy house. Maybe they wouldn't even have let them in."

Oscar: "The shepherds wouldn't even have wanted to go there because they would have seen he wasn't coming for them but for the rich."

I said: "And the rich don't need liberation. What liberation do the rich need!"

William: "The rich need to be liberated from their money."

Felipe: "When the poor get liberated, they'll get liberated too."

Little Adan: "The poor will liberate them."

Francisco: "And the poor also have the chance to be great, like the Messiah who was born like the common people."

I said: "The people really have great abilities that

only need to be developed. When the people have education, enough food . . ."

NATALIA: "Like in Cuba, where all the children are healthy. They're all taken care of when they're sick and everything. If you're old they take care of you. They give you everything you need and you're healthy and eager to work. And there the poor can learn a profession. And where can anybody do that here?"

And suddenly next to the angel appeared many other angels from heaven praising God, and saying, "Glory to God in the highest; and on earth peace to men who love."

Old TOMAS PEÑA asked: "Those other angels who had stayed behind, who didn't come with the other angel, was it because God hadn't enlightened them yet, or was it because they had to come farther?"

I said: "Or because the shepherds hadn't seen them First an angel speaks to them, afterwards they hear others. . . ."

TOMAS: "It's like us here. We're all listening, but we don't manage to understand everything. So then, those who had heard hadn't taken it all in."

DON JULIO CHAVARRIA: "Not until that moment was there peace on earth—when the child was born. And that's probably why there was joy in heaven. That's what the angels are singing, it seems to me."

Goodness and Light

EDGARD, a young man who had been a Franciscan and who was visiting us, said: "The glory of God can't exist in heaven until there is peace among men, which means justice, brotherhood, equality (peace is all this). The rich often believe that they give glory to God, but they don't give peace and justice, and so they don't give glory to God because the two things go together."

WILLIAM: "When there is peace, love, there is glory to God."

They went quickly and found Mary and Joseph, and the child lying in the manger. When they saw him, they told what the angel had said to them about the child, and all those who heard them wondered at what they said.

JULIO: "Before they felt oppressed, and when the Savior came, they felt free and told about their joy."

TOMAS: "And then all the people were happy, I mean the poor people, because the new news reached them all."

But Mary kept all this in her heart, thinking about it.

TOMAS: "She wasn't surprised like the rest of them, because she was lit up by the Holy Spirit and by everything that had happened to her. But even so she thought that maybe others would tell things that weren't so. They would make them bigger and say things they hadn't seen. And she also thought that they could kill him, or do something else to him, right? Dangerous. . . . They could do all kinds of bad things to him."

I: "Yes, Mary already knew from the Annunciation that Jesus would be the Messiah. . . ."

TOMAS: "She thought they could hurt him because he was the Messiah. And they did attack him. Because since he was coming to liberate us, all the people, he would face many enemies. He was going to have many struggles."

JULIO: "And if Mary knew that's why Jesus was coming, and she knew it sooner than the angels, why didn't she tell? Why did she wait for the angels to tell? It seems to me she was afraid they would come to kill him, so she'd rather keep the secret. That's why she didn't tell."

OSCAR: "The shepherds knew it. The king and the rich people didn't know it. The same thing happens now. Not everybody knows about the coming of this Jesus."

JULIO: "I think a lot of people know about it, but what happens is that there's a lot of fear. They don't dare approach like the shepherds did because they're afraid. And there are a lot of other people who don't know about it."

Missa Cantata

Evelyn Underhill

Once in an abbey-church, the while we prayed,
All silent at the lifting of the Host,
A little bird through some high window strayed,
And to and fro
Like a wee angel lost
That on a sudden finds its heaven below,
It went the morning long
And made our Eucharist more glad with song.

It sang, it sang! And as the quiet priest
Far off about the lighted altar moved,
The awful substance of the mystic feast
All hushed before
It like a thing that loved,

Yet loved in liberty, would plunge and soar
Beneath the vault in play
And thence toss down the oblation of its lay.

The walls that went our sanctuary around
Did as of old, to that sweet summons yield.
New scents and sounds within our gates were found,
The cry of kine,
The fragrance of the field,
All woodland whispers, hastened to the shrine,
The country side was come
Eager and joyful, to its spirit's home.

Far stretched I saw the cornfield and the plough,
The scudding cloud, the cleanly running brook,
The humble kindly turf, the tossing bough,
That all their light
From Love's own furnace took,
This altar, where one angel brownly bright
Proclaimed the sylvan creed,
And sang the Benedictus of the mead.

All earth was lifted to communion then,
All lovely life was there to meet its King;
Ah, not the little arid souls of men

GOODNESS AND LIGHT

But sun and wind
And all desirous thing
The ground of their beseeching here did find;
All with one self same bread,
And all by one eternal priest were fed.

If Christ Had Become Incarnate Now

Oscar Romero

If Christ had become incarnate now
and were a thirty-year-old man today,
he would be here in the cathedral
and we wouldn't know him from the rest of you—
a thirty-year-old man, a peasant from Nazareth,
here in the cathedral like any peasant
from our countryside.
The Son of God made flesh would be here
and we wouldn't know him—
one completely like us.

How shameful to think that perhaps pagans,
people with no faith in Christ,
may be better than we
and nearer to God's reign.
Remember how Christ received a pagan centurion
and told him, "I'll go and cure your servant"?
The centurion, full of humility and confidence,
said, "No, Lord, I am not worthy that you go there.
Just say a word
and my servant will be cured."
Christ marveled, says the gospel, and he said,
"Truly, I have not found such faith in Israel."
I say:
Christ will also say of this church:
outside the limits of Catholicism
perhaps there is more faith,
more holiness.
So we must not extinguish the Spirit.
The Spirit is not the monopoly of a movement,
even of a Christian movement,
of a hierarchy, or priesthood, or religious
congregation.
The Spirit is free,
and he wants men and women,
wherever they are,

to realize their vocation to find Christ,
who became flesh to save all human flesh.
Yes, to save all, dear brothers and sisters.
I know that some people come to the cathedral
who have even lost the faith and are non-Christians.
Let them be welcome.
And if this message is saying something to them,
I ask them to reflect in their inner consciousness,
for, like Christ, I can tell them:
the kingdom of God is not far from you,
God's kingdom is within your heart.
Seek it, and you will find it.

The Bible has a very meaningful expression:
The Spirit makes all things new.
We are those who grow old,
and we want everyone made to our aged pattern.
The Spirit is never old,
the Spirit is always young.

Remembering the Sacred Presence of the One Who Dwells among Us

Joyce Rupp

May we look for your goodness in people who seem least likely to carry your love.

May we behold your radiance in the ones we quickly pass by at home or work.

May we discover your love in our deeper self when we feel unloving and irritable.

May we embrace you in the persons whose faithfulness we take for granted.

May we see your empathy in those serving the wounded of the world.

May we recognize your courage in the valiant people who speak out for justice.

May we notice your non-judgmental acceptance in those who keep an open mind.

May we search for your gentleness when it is covered with harshness in another.

May we observe your generosity in every gift we receive, no matter how small it is.

May we reveal your mercy when we pardon someone for having turned against us.

May we welcome your joy in the delightful voices and happy play of children.

May we convey your compassion when we visit those with illness and poor health.

May we detect your patience in those who put up with our impatience and hurry.

May we unite with your peace hidden beneath the layers of the world's disharmony.

O Divine One, you came into our world in the form of a newly emerged child, fresh and fragile as all of us at our birthing. You came as a beloved one filled with the radiance of eternal Light. As you grew in humanness, your life and teachings revealed the vast goodness of your inner being. We now carry your loving Spirit of radiance within us. We can easily miss this gift in the press of our activities and our clouded, inner vision. Skim away the inattentiveness of our minds and the crusts of unloving on our hearts. As we prepare to celebrate the wonder of your birth, help us discern your concealed presence in each part of our life.

⇗

Epiphany: Goodness and Light

Kathy McNeely

*Nations shall come to see your light, and kings
to the brightness of your dawn.*

—Isaiah 60:3

"Arise, shine; for your light has come," proclaims Isaiah, referring to a time when people who had once been dispersed gather again in goodness and light. It's the dawn of a new age, a new time in history where things are radically different from the past. The feast of Epiphany has always fascinated me because it is a celebration of a very new way in which God interacts with human history—and it comes about through the participation of a starry night that signals to visitors from afar, as well as to shepherds in nearby hills, to come and see the new thing that God was doing in the birth of Jesus. It is through their profound un-derstanding of (and connection to) the natural world that both the Magi and the shepherds were able to read nature's signs and know God's revelation. And through them, Herod—the figurehead of the Jewish people—came to know that something new (and very threatening) was about to happen.

When I lived and worked in Guatemala I would often sit outside at night and gaze at the stars. The town where I lived had little (sometimes no) elec-tricity, so the sky was teeming with a thick coat of stars, many more stars than I ever remembered see-ing in my hometown of Cleveland, Ohio. In another instance, during a visit to missioners in South Su-dan, one evening we sat out in the middle of a nearby field to gaze at the stars. With no moon, we needed flashlights to walk out to the place where we chose to sit. While stargazing I heard someone running by. I could hardly believe what I heard. The Sudanese man moving at full speed was so accustomed to the dark that he could navigate the uneven and thorny terrain running in bare feet. Since I grew up accus-tomed to light bulbs, I could never imagine having such keen eyesight at night.

Today's reading, having provoked these memories,

prompted me to think about the way that the Magi and the shepherds read the sky like a textbook. I knew that Guatemalan farmers did the same thing. It's the stars, the planets and the shape of the moon that tell them exactly when to plant or when to harvest their crops. I know that it was true for the people of South Sudan as well. They can determine the best places to go to graze their animals by what the moon and stars say. Many of us who live in more industrialized cities in the northern hemisphere have stopped looking to nature for information, and we really do not often include the natural world in a lot of our decision making.

In the fall of 2012 Hurricane Sandy reminded people living on the U.S.'s east coast how important it is not take nature for granted. Sandy showed us that storms have gained intensity in recent years and that many of our cities are built in precarious places, like a tiny island that juts out into a big ocean.

Sandy and other signs of stress that the natural world now shows invite me to wonder whether we are at just such a time as the one the Isaiah was announcing. Perhaps we can begin to look at the new things that God is doing in human history, and more centrally at how God acts on this very earth. Today those of us from the global North are invited to consider seriously the consequences of trying to subdue nature for our own gain—over and above the notion of working with nature to meet human needs as practiced by the people of the deserts of South Sudan or the jungles of Guatemala.

Matthew's Gospel describing Jesus' birth and his first visitors reminds us of the way that God really turns things upside down. It is the wealthy wise men from the east who come and bow down before a child whose family looks like they are the outcasts of society. The shepherds, often reviled for illegally grazing on other people's lands, are also there—right alongside the wealthy foreigners—the first to recognize and to celebrate God's breaking through history. And Herod, the guy who's supposed to be in charge—and know everything that's going on with the Jewish people—is left in the dark, and wondering how long he might maintain his power.

We have so much to learn. Through Epiphany we are invited not only to think about how well we care for one another—our "fellow heirs, members of the same body, and sharers in the promise in Christ Jesus through the gospel" (Ephesians 3:6). We must also learn how to live on this Earth, and to learn all Earth's wonderful ways of communicating. After all, we might not even have a gift-giving tradition to cel-ebrate Christmas if the Magi were not busy reading nature's signs and charting their path accordingly!

Sources and Acknowledgments

NOVEMBER 21: "Advent," from Thomas Merton, *The Wisdom of the Desert*. Copyright © 1986 by John Allman. Reprinted by permission of New Directions Publishing Corp.

NOVEMBER 22: "Salvation Army Santa Claus Clangs His Bell," from "Advent," in Frederick Buechner, *Whistling in the Dark*. Copyright © 1988, 1993 by Frederick Buechner. Reprinted by permission of HarperCollins Publishers.

NOVEMBER 23: "What Are You Waiting For?," by Robert Barron, originally appeared in the December 2003 (Volume 68, Number 12) issue of *U.S. Catholic*. Reprinted by permission of U.S. Catholic magazine, published by the Claretians, www.uscatholic.org.

NOVEMBER 24: "Christmas Time in Bolivia" by Maggie Fogarty, is reprinted from *A Maryknoll Liturgical Year: Reflections on the Readings for Year B*, Orbis Books, 2014.

NOVEMBER 25: "Less Is More" is reprinted from Richard Rohr, *Preparing for Christmas: Daily Meditations for Advent*, Franciscan Media, 2008.

NOVEMBER 26: "Christmas Is a Sad Season for the Poor," by John Cheever, from *The Stories of John Cheever*. Copyright © 1978 by John Cheever. Used by permission of Alfred A. Knopf, an imprint of the Knopf Doubleday Publishing Group, a division of Random House LLC. All rights reserved.

NOVEMBER 27: "Christmas to Me," by Harper Lee, was originally published in *McCall's* in December 1961. Reprinted by permission of Andrew Nurnberg Associates, London.

Sources and Acknowledgments

NOVEMBER 28: "Magnificat," by Joelle Chase, appeared in *Spectrum Magazine*, December 11, 2011. Reprinted by permission of *Spectrum Magazine*, www.spectrummagazine.org.

NOVEMBER 29: "Soda Bread in Tanzania," by Patricia Gallogly, MM, is reprinted from *A Maryknoll Liturgical Year: Reflections on the Readings for Year B*, Orbis Books, 2014.

NOVEMBER 30: "The Time Machine," copyright © 2006 by Anna Quindlen was originally published in *Newsweek*, December 2006. Used by permission. All rights reserved.

DECEMBER 1: "Mary Christ Bus," by Brian Doyle, is reprinted by permission of the author.

DECEMBER 2: "The Burglar's Christmas," by Willa Cather, is reprinted by permission of the Willa Cather Literary Trust.

DECEMBER 3: "The Smell of Sheep," is reprinted from Carlo Carretto, *Blessed are You Who Believed*, Orbis Books, 1983.

DECEMBER 4: "Advent Is about Desire" is adapted from *The Jesuit Guide to (Almost) Everything*. Copyright © 2010 by James Martin, SJ. Reprinted by permission of HarperCollins Publishers.

DECEMBER 5: "Christ in Cambodia," by Maria Montello, is reprinted from *A Maryknoll Liturgical Year: Reflections on the Readings for Year B*, Orbis Books, 2014.

DECEMBER 6: "Asking for a Sign," by Alan Jones, is reprinted by permission of the author.

DECEMBER 7: "Advent in Peru," by Larry Rich, is reprinted from *A Maryknoll Liturgical Year: Reflections on the Readings for Year B*, Orbis Books, 2014.

DECEMBER 8: "A Familiar, Sweet Hunger," by Phyllis Tickle, is used by permission of the author.

DECEMBER 9: "Advent" appeared in *Open Shutters: Poems by Mary Jo Salter*, copyright © 2003 by Mary Jo Salter. Used by permission of

December 10: "Would It Be Okay if You Hugged Me? What a Tearful Teenage Boy Taught Me about Advent," by Sarah Thebarge, from *Sojourners*, December 2013. Reprinted with permission from *Sojourners*, (800) 714-7474, www.sojo.net.

December 11: "One or Two Things about Christmas," appeared in Annie Dillard, *Tickets for a Prayer Wheel*. Copyright © 2002 by Annie Dillard. Reprinted by permission of Wesleyan University Press.

December 12: "Expectation of Our Blessed Mother," is an excerpt from an address given by Mother Mary Joseph Rogers to the Maryknoll Sisters on December 22, 1949, at Maryknoll, NY.

December 13: "True Happiness," is an excerpt from *Alfred Delp: Prison Writings*, Orbis Books, 2004.

December 14: "Be Vigilant at All Times," by David Davis, from *Naked and You Clothed Me: Homilies and Reflections for Cycle A*, Jim Knipper ed., Clear Faith Publishing, 2013.

December 15: "The Materialism of Santa Claus and the Spirituality of Baby Jesus," by Leonardo Boff, is reprinted by permission of the author.

December 16: "The Jesus I Love," is an excerpt from Mohandas Gandhi, *Young India, December 31, 1931*, reprinted by permission of Navajivan Trust, Ahmedabad, India.

December 17: "Christmas in Prison," by Pedro Arrupe, from "Eucharist and Youth," *Other Apostolates Today*. St. Louis: Institute of Jesuit Sources, 1981. Used with permission: Copyright © 1981. The Institute of Jesuit Sources, St. Louis, MO. All rights reserved.

December 18: A version of "The Surprise Child," by James T. Keane, was originally published in *America* on December 10, 2007. Used with permission of the author.

Sources and Acknowledgments

DECEMBER 19: "The Miracle of Christmas Bread," by Rose Marie Berger, was originally published in *Sojourners*, January 2014. Reprinted with permission from *Sojourners*, (800) 714-7474, www.sojo.net.

DECEMBER 20: "Do Not Be Afraid" by Greg Kandra, from *Naked and You Clothed Me: Homilies and Reflections for Cycle A,* Jim Knipper ed., Clear Faith Publishing, 2013.

DECEMBER 21: "Into the Dark with God," is an excerpt from Hans Urs von Balthasar, *You Crown the Year with Your Goodness: Sermons Throughout the Liturgical Year*, Ignatius Press, 1989. Reprinted by permission of Ignatius Press.

DECEMBER 22: "Christmas Poem" appears in *Twelve Moons: Poems by Mary Oliver*. Copyright © 1979 by Mary Oliver. Used by permission of Little Brown and Company.

DECEMBER 23: "Christmas Eve Vigil," by Kathleen Norris, is reprinted from *God With Us*, Greg Pennoyer & Gregory Wolfe, eds. Copyright © 2007 by Greg Pennoyer. Used with permission of Paraclete Press, www.paracletepress.com.

DECEMBER 24: "A Burst of Brilliant Light" is an excerpt from Pope Francis's Midnight Mass homily on December 24, 2013, "Solemnity of the Nativity of the Lord." Copyright © 2013 Libreria Editrice Vaticana. Used by permission of Libreria Editrice Vaticana.

DECEMBER 25: "Have a Defiant Christmas!," by John Shea, is used by permission of the author.

DECEMBER 26: "The Birth of Jesus" is an excerpt from Mary Christine Athans, *In Quest of the Jewish Mary*, Orbis Books, 2013.

DECEMBER 27: "Christmas Confession," by Anne Rice. Copyright © 2010 by Anne O'Brien Rice. Used by permission of the author.

DECEMBER 28: "Papa Panov's Special Christmas," by Leo Tolstoy is based on a story in French by Ruben Saillens and was adapted and translated by Leo Tolstoy.

December 29: "Holy Innocents" is an excerpt from Robert Ellsberg, *All Saints: Daily Reflections on Saints, Prophets, and Witnesses for Our Time*. Copyright © 1997 by Robert Ellsberg. New York: The Crossroad Publishing Company.

December 30: "Jesus the Worker" is an excerpt from Walter J. Ciszek, *He Leadeth Me*. Copyright © 1973 by Walter J. Ciszek. San Francisco: Ignatius Press, 1995.

December 31: "Christmas for Mystics," is taken from Marianne Williamson's December 12, 2012, blog, at www.marianne.com. Reprinted by permission of Marianne Williamson.

January 1: "In Congo or Croydon, God Is There for Us," an article by Archbishop Rowan Williams based on his experience in Eastern Congo during June 2011, was published in *The Times* newspaper on December 24, 2011. Reprinted by permission of Dr. Rowan Williams.

January 2: "Amazing Peace" from *Amazing Peace: A Christmas Poem* by Maya Angelou. Copyright © 2005 by Maya Angelou. Used by permission of Random House, an imprint and division of Random House LLC. All rights reserved.

January 3: "The Shepherds of Bethlehem" is an excerpt from Ernesto Cardenal, *The Gospel in Solentiname*, Orbis Books, 2010.

January 4: "Missa Cantata" is an excerpt from Evelyn Underhill, *Immanence: A Book of Verses,* 1920.

January 5: "If Christ Had Become Incarnate Now" is an excerpt from Oscar Romero, *The Violence of Love*. Copyright © 1988 by the Chicago Province of the Society of Jesus, Orbis Books, 2004.

January 6: "Remembering the Sacred Presence of the One Who Dwells Among Us," by Joyce Rupp, is used by permission of the author.

January 7: Kathy McNeely, "Epiphany: Goodness and Light" reprinted from *A Maryknoll Liturgical Year: Reflections on the Readings for Year B*, Orbis Books, 2014.

INDEX OF CONTRIBUTORS

Maya Angelou (d. 2014) is the author of seven autobiographies, three books of essays, and several books of poetry, as well as a number of plays and television and movie scripts. Angelou is best known for her autobiographies, including *I Know Why the Caged Bird Sings* (1969).
. . . . *January 2*

Pedro Arrupe, SJ (d. 1991) was the Superior General of the Society of Jesus from 1965 to 1983. He was imprisoned for a time by the Japanese during World War II, and was a survivor of the American atomic attack on Hiroshima. Sometimes called the "Second Founder" of the Jesuits, he oversaw the order's shift to a greater commitment to social justice after Vatican I.. . . . . *December 17*

Mary Christine Athans, BVM, is a Sister of Charity of the Blessed Virgin Mary and the author of *In Quest of the Jewish Mary*. She is professor emerita at the Saint Paul Seminary School of Divinity of the University of St. Thomas (Minnesota) . . . . *December 26*

Robert Barron is a Catholic priest of the Archdiocese of Chicago and the Rector of Mundelein Seminary. An acclaimed author and speaker, he is also the founder of Word on Fire Catholic Ministries. . . . . *November 23*

Rose Marie Berger is a social activist, author, and senior associate editor at *Sojourners* magazine. She is the author of *Drawn By God: A History of the Society of Catholic Medical Missionaries from 1967 to 1991* and *Who Killed Donte Manning? The Story of an American Neighborhood* . . . . *December 19*

Goodness and Light

Leonardo Boff is a Brazilian theologian considered to be one of the founders of liberation theology. He has written more than eighty books, including *Jesus Christ Liberator, Christianity in a Nutshell,* and *Francis of Rome, Francis of Assisi.* . . . . *December 15*

Frederick Buechner is an American theologian and author. He has been a finalist for the Pulitzer Prize and the National Book Award, and has written over thirty books of fiction, essays, memoir, and sermons. . . . .*November 22*

Ernesto Cardenal is a Nicaraguan Catholic priest, liberation theologian, and poet, as well as the founder of Solentiname, a primitivist art community. He served as Nicaragua's minister of culture from 1979 to 1987. . . . . *January 3*

Carlo Carretto (d. 1988) was a member of the Little Brothers of Jesus, an order inspired by the spirituality of Charles de Foucauld. He lived in the Sahara Desert of Algeria for ten years, and twenty years later wrote *Letters from the Desert,* a popular vision of a new kind of contemplative life in the world. He went on to publish a dozen other books. . . . . *December 3*

Willa Cather (d. 1947) was an American author who wrote extensively of life on the Great Plains. Her many novels include *O Pioneers!, My Ántonia, Death Comes for the Archbishop,* and *One of Ours,* for which she received the Pulitzer Prize in 1923. . . . . *December 2*

Joelle Chase is Director of Messaging for the Center for Action and Contemplation (an ecumenical, educational non-profit). She lives in Albuquerque, New Mexico. . . . .*November 28*

John Cheever (d. 1982) was a short story writer and novelist recognized as one of the most important fiction writers of the twentieth century. "The Chekhov of the suburbs," Cheever is famous for his fictional treatment of the themes of alienation and community in American life.. . . . .*November 26*

Walter Ciszek, SJ (d. 1984), was an American Jesuit priest sent as a missionary to the Soviet Union. After being captured, he spent more than twenty years in confinement and hard labor before he was released and returned to the United States in 1963. He is the author of *He Leadeth Me* and *With God in Russia*.

David A. Davis is the senior pastor of the Nassau Presbyterian Church in Princeton, New Jersey. A contributor to various journals in the discipline of preaching, he has published of a collection of his sermons: *A Kingdom You Can Taste: Sermons for the Church Year*.

Alfred Delp, SJ (d. 1945), was a German Jesuit executed by the Nazis for anti-Hitler activities. During his months in prison he composed a series of now-famous meditations on Advent, the Lord's Prayer, the tasks of the future, the meaning of happiness, and other spiritual themes.

Annie Dillard is a well-known American author of poetry, essays, literary criticism, novels, and memoir. She taught for twenty-one years in the English department of Wesleyan University, in Middletown, Connecticut. She won the Pulitzer Prize for General Nonfiction in 1974 for her book *Pilgrim at Tinker Creek*.

Brian Doyle is the editor of *Portland Magazine* and the author of many books, notably the novels *Mink River* and *The Plover*. His work has appeared in *The Atlantic Monthly*, *Harper's*, *The New York Times*, and in many other periodicals around the world.

Robert Ellsberg is the editor-in-chief and publisher of Orbis Books. He is the author of numerous books, including *All Saints* and *The Saints' Guide to Happiness*.

Maggie Fogarty is the co-director of the NH Program of the American Friends Service Committee (AFSC). She is also a community organizer, public policy advocate, educator, and coalition builder on a variety of issues including affordable housing, homelessness, and the rights of workers, tenants, immigrants, and refugees. She served as a Maryknoll Lay Missioner in Bolivia.

Goodness and Light

Pope Francis, the former archbishop of Buenos Aires, was elected on March 13, 2013.............................. *December 24*

Patricia Gallogly, MM, is a Maryknoll sister who served for many years in Tanzania in primary and secondary schools.
....*November 29*

Mohandas Gandhi (d. 1948) was the foremost leader in the Indian independence movement during and after World War II. Assassinated in 1948, he is best-known for his teachings on active non-violent resistance, which have inspired similar actions and movements throughout the world. .... *December 16*

Alan Jones is an author and a prominent lecturer both nationally and internationally on spirituality and theology. He was the Dean of Grace Cathedral in San Francisco from 1985 until 2009 and a professor at General Theological Seminary in New York City from 1972 to 1982................................. *December 6*

Greg Kandra is a Roman Catholic deacon serving the Diocese of Brooklyn, New York. He worked for twenty-six years as a writer and producer for CBS News in both New York and Washington. He is the creator of "The Deacon's Bench" blog and is the multimedia editor for the Catholic Near East Welfare Association.
....*December 20*

James T. Keane is an editor at Orbis Books and a columnist for *America Magazine*. His writing has also appeared in *Busted Halo, Catholic Digest, Hypothetical Review, Philadelphia Weekly, Popoli,* and *U.S. Catholic.*................................... *December 18*

Harper Lee is an American novelist best known for her 1960 novel *To Kill A Mockingbird* for which she was awarded the Pulitzer Prize in 1961. ....*November 27*

James Martin, SJ, is a Jesuit priest, an editor at *America Magazine*, and a well-known American spiritual writer. He is a frequent media commentator and was the "official chaplain" of *The Colbert Report*.
....*December 4*

Index of Contributors

Richard Rohr, OFM, is a Franciscan priest and founder of the Center for Action and Contemplation. A globally recognized ecumenical teacher, he is the author of numerous books on faith, spirituality, and mysticism. . . . . *November 25*

Oscar Romero (d. 1980) was the archbishop of San Salvador. Assassinated in 1980 for his public denunciations of poverty, social injustice, assassinations, and torture in El Salvador, he is revered by many in El Salvador and beyond as a saint. In 1997, Pope John Paul II named him a Servant of God, and his cause for beatification and canonization is open. . . . . *January 5*

Joyce Rupp is the author of numerous books, including *Open the Door, Fragments of Your Ancient Name, The Cosmic Dance, Prayer,* and *Walk in a Relaxed Manner.* She is a member of the Servite (Servants of Mary) community and the co-director of the Institute of Compassionate Presence. . . . . *January 6*

Mary Jo Salter is the author of seven books of poetry, most recently *Nothing by Design.* A frequent reviewer and essayist, she is also a lyricist whose song cycle, "Rooms of Light," premiered at Lincoln Center in 2007. As well, she is co-editor of the fourth and fifth editions of *The Norton Anthology of Poetry.* . . . . *December 9*

John Shea is a theologian and author of numerous books, including *Following Jesus, The Legend of the Bells and Other Stories,* and *Gospel Light.*
. . . . *December 25*

Sarah Thebarge is a lecturer and author. In 2013 she published a memoir of her experiences with a Somali refugee family, *The Invisible Girls.* Her writing has also appeared in *Everyday Health, Relevant Magazine, BurnsideWriters.com, Christianity Today, Sojo.net, Red Letter Christian,* and *Huffington Post.* . . . . *December 10*

Phyllis Tickle is the author of over three dozen books on religion and spirituality and a prominent lecturer on religion in America. She is the founding editor of the Religion Department of *Publishers Weekly.* . . . . *December 8*